Mariam,
Best wishes in y'
independence!

Sincerely,
Dan

The Richest Doctor - A Modern Parable of Financial Independence

ISBN: 978-0-578-36526-8 (Hardback)

ISBN: 979-8-9859677-0-8 (Paperback)

ISBN: 979-8-9859677-1-5 (Digital)

Disclaimer

The material in this publication is of the nature of general comment only, and does not represent professional advice. It is not intended to provide specific guidance for particular circumstances and it should not be relied on as the basis for any decision to take action or not take action on any matter which it covers.

Readers should obtain professional advice where appropriate, before making any such decision.

To the maximum extent permitted by law, the author and publisher disclaim all responsibility and liability to any person, arising directly or indirectly from any person taking or not taking action based on the information in the publication.

Also by David Auer

Ignite Your Life with Brian Tracy

Performance 360 Special Edition with Richard Branson

Road to Success with Jack Canfield

57 Ways to Grow Your Business - Bright Ideas for Serious Entrepreneurs

You Can Deduct That?

10 Most Expensive Tax Mistakes That Cost Business Owners Thousands

The Great Tax Escape -
Strategies for Early Planning and Beating the System (of the IRS)

The Richest Doctor

A Modern Parable of Financial Independence

David Auer

CPA, MS, PFS, CGMA, JD, LLM in Taxation

For my wife Julia and children, Ellen, Emily, and John.

Also, to the physicians I've met along the way that have helped me understand their needs, their goals, and how to convey the important steps that build to financial independence.

Contents

Preface 7

Foreword 9

Introduction 11

Chapter 1: The Gathering 14

Chapter 2: The Counselor 22

Chapter 3: The Journey Begins 30
    Step 1: Develop a Written Plan 30
    Step 2: Reduce Taxes 37
    Step 3: Control Cash Flow 55
    Step 4: Seek Wise Counsel 69
    Step 5: Understand Risk 72
    Step 6: Build Tax-Efficient Wealth 72

Chapter 4: Five Years Later 85
    Step 7: Focus on Progress, Not Perfection 99

Chapter 5: The 10-Year Reunion 103
    Step 8: Keep Perspective 110

Chapter 6: Epilogue 114

Chapter 7: Getting Started 117

Preface

When I was eleven years old, I started my first job as a newspaper carrier in a small town in Kansas. I learned a lot about how businesses ran at that early age.

I was lucky. I took over the paper route that my older sister had, so I had a good mentor to show me what to do and what not to do. That business taught me about taking responsibility, providing excellent customer service, and keeping accurate financial records.

The strong work ethic, as well as sound financial and business principles, I learned at the age of 11 has carried on throughout my life. I never went without a job – all the way through high school, undergraduate and graduate school, law school and graduate law school. I didn't have parents who were business owners – my father was an engineer, and my mother was a schoolteacher. While they didn't teach me about business, they did teach me the value of education and continual lifetime learning.

I was also influenced by many wise counselors and advisors. When I was a Certified Public Accountant (CPA) working for a national accounting firm in Dallas, my future father-in-law advised me that if I learned to study the law by pursuing a law degree and a graduate tax law degree, I could acquire the rare but highly valuable ability to view the tax law both quantitatively as a CPA and qualitatively as a tax attorney. He was an estate planning attorney, so it seemed like great advice.

So that's what I did, and along the way, picked up several credentials – including becoming a Certified Tax Coach, Certified Tax Strategist, Personal Financial Specialist, and Chartered Global Management Accountant. I also shared my acquired experiences by writing or co-authoring several books about tax, financial, and business planning. It was always my goal to be the best tax advisor possible for my clients.

When I founded Physician Tax Solutions, a division of Provident CPAs PLC, focusing on proactive tax, financial, and business advisory services for our niche client, who we describe as an "ambitious entrepreneurial doctor," I realized while working with hundreds of entrepreneurial doctors that our backgrounds of work ethic and lifetime learning were very similar. We work with physicians, dentists, veterinarians, chiropractors, and other high-income professionals to help them become financially independent as early as possible.

We define "financial independence" as having enough investible assets that generate annual passive income that replaces the amount of active income needed to provide the lifestyle you desire. Helping our clients achieve financial independence is the "why" Provident CPAs exists – it's our purpose and reason for being.

I'm very proud of the passion our team has every day serving our clients, and the client-oriented culture we've created. Most of our clients are like family to us – we know their children's names and celebrate their birthdays and anniversaries. Together, we've gone through thick and thin, good times and bad times, including the COVID-19 pandemic. Perhaps most importantly, our team members show up every day looking for ways to save our clients money and reduce taxes, thus helping them achieve financial independence as early as possible.

Foreword

I think most people reading this book are generally looking for the same thing — Freedom.

There are many ideas about what freedom entails, but financial freedom is the foundation of all personal freedoms. From the time I was young, I wanted to be a surgeon. There were several significant events that led me to this career goal, including family illnesses and my own injuries as an athlete. Like so many of my medical colleagues, I came from a background that rewarded hard work, but no one in my family had achieved professional or financial success. We were a blue-collar family of construction workers, union employees, truck drivers, and plumbers. There was a strong history of military service in my family that I continued myself. I am honored and proud of that background.

As I approached my goal of becoming a surgeon, I looked at the costs associated with obtaining the necessary education. It is not uncommon for my peers to have over $300,000 in loan debt after undergraduate and medical school. For this reason, I chose to use the Health Professions Scholarship Program with the Army to help afford these costs. This led to some of the greatest life experiences and friendships that I will ever have.

After finishing residency and serving out my time, I completed a fellowship in Adult Reconstruction at New England Baptist Hospital in Boston. When that year was completed, I was 36 years old and taking my first civilian job as an orthopedic surgeon in my hometown. I was married with two children and one on the way. I had been practicing independently for four years prior to the fellowship and felt a profound sense of delayed gratification when we bought our home in Tulsa.

Like many, I bought a home that was bigger and fancier than I needed because I felt I had worked and waited for it, and now we deserved it. But to be honest, I had little in the way of savings and my budget was not in check. I had always thought someday I will make a lot of money and I can make up for it. I am sure that many of my colleagues have similar stories.

Although I had gained an enormous wealth of medical knowledge over the prior decade, I failed to educate myself financially. Fortunately for me, I met David Auer through a friend in 2017. We discussed my situation, much like what happens in the parable you are about to read.

My initial goals were to limit my tax burden, start saving for retirement, fund my children's education, and ultimately learn ways to start growing our wealth. What has occurred while working with David and his team has truly changed my life. We have committed to the strategies that are in this book. I find myself stepping in and out of Self-employed, Business Owner, and Investor boxes, with the ultimate goal of being financially independent in the next decade. I have gained a great deal of knowledge since working with David and his team and that education continues today. The process takes self-control, a willingness to budget, and a commitment to constantly reassess. But I am a testament to the process. I encourage all reading this book to seek wise counsel and commit themselves to becoming financially free.

J. Scott Reid, M.D.
Tulsa Bone and Joint Associates
Tulsa, Okla.

Introduction

So why did you become a doctor? No doubt, you have been asked that question dozens of times.

Was it to help others in a very important way by improving their health?

Was it because of the honor and respect associated with the health-care profession?

Was it because medicine was fascinating and challenging?

Or was it to become financially independent? I doubt many of you did it solely because of the financial possibilities.

You don't need to feel guilty if one of your reasons to become a doctor was or is to be able to provide for yourself and your family and be financially comfortable.

This book is written as a parable about four doctors – Elijah, Serena, Ben, and Indira – who are close friends from medical school. They met up at a medical conference five years after completing their residency in emergency medicine. The friends collectively share their frustration of not being further ahead financially at this stage of their career. They decide to meet with Will, a veteran CPA and serial entrepreneur, who works with Indira's parents. Will helps the doctors create a plan and guides them on their individual journeys to financial independence.

The Richest Doctor is a brilliantly simple and encouraging story of lessons to build financial intelligence, develop a long-term plan to achieve financial independence, get control of cash flow, reduce taxes, understand investment risk, and seek wise counsel. The book tracks each of the doctors' progress over 25 years, as each doctor pursues their dreams of becoming financially independent.

The Richest Doctor becomes enriched in their purpose. "Rich" doesn't just mean having money, it applies to a life well lived with purpose.

The Richest Doctor knows their reason for becoming a doctor and being disciplined to be a good steward of their financial lives. What does financial independence mean to you?

My definition of financial independence is – "having the financial freedom to do what I want when I want, the way I want, with whom I want in a manner I want."

The healthcare industry is amid crises of burnout and financial stress as compensation levels are continually pressed downward by the insurance industry and government regulation. *The Richest Doctor* provides a roadmap for doctors to escape the "rat race" to become financially free from these pressures.

Also, please note that the tax strategies mentioned in the book were provided under the tax code circa 2021. While much of the advice within this story is timeless, some strategies could become dated. It's always best to work with a knowledgeable, proactive tax strategist and compliance team for the most up-to-date strategies.

A Lesson from Robert Frost

My favorite poem is "The Road Not Taken" by Robert Frost. It has been an inspiration to me in writing this book, and I hope it is an inspiration likewise to you as you read this book.

The Road Not Taken

Two roads diverged in a yellow wood,
And sorry I could not travel both
And be one traveler, long I stood
And looked down one as far as I could
To where it bent in the undergrowth;

Then took the other, as just as fair,
And having perhaps the better claim,
Because it was grassy and wanted wear;
Though as for that the passing there
Had worn them really about the same,

And both that morning equally lay
In leaves no step had trodden black.
Oh, I kept the first for another day!
Yet knowing how way leads on to way,
I doubted if I should ever come back.

I shall be telling this with a sigh
Somewhere ages and ages hence:
Two roads diverged in a wood, and I—
I took the one less traveled by,
And that has made all the difference.

Chapter 1
The Gathering

The alarm went off at 5 a.m. Elijah woke up with a start.

"Where am I?" he thought to himself as he looked around the hotel room.

After a few moments, his mind cleared, and he remembered he had flown in late the night before to attend the four-day Rocky Mountain Trauma & Emergency Medicine Conference in Denver. It was rare for Elijah to spend the night away from his home in Oklahoma City, where he lived with his wife, Joy, and their four children, ages 2, 4, 6, and 8. He was startled to wake up in a place besides his home or the back room of the hospital's emergency room, where he would catch a nap occasionally between patients and writing reports.

As was his normal routine after a short night of sleep, Elijah immediately looked for the coffee maker in order to get a jolt of caffeine to jump-start his brain.

Elijah and Joy had made the decision early in their marriage that Joy, a registered nurse by training, would stay at home raising their children, and he would be the sole breadwinner for the family. Although their living expenses were high, Elijah was able to pick up extra shifts at the hospital. That extra income allowed them to afford a nice family vacation several times a year and live in an affluent neighborhood in the suburbs near Elijah's parents.

Elijah's father was a tenured professor teaching chemistry and biology at the University of Central Oklahoma, and Elijah's mother worked for the Oklahoma Department of Health and Human Services. Both had worked for the same organizations for almost 40 years and were within a few years of retirement. They looked forward to the opportunity to travel and spend more time with their grandchildren, knowing that they could live comfortably on their government retirement plans.

About the same time as Elijah was waking, Serena was finishing her shift as a physician working in the emergency room at a large hospital in Kansas City, Missouri. She had packed her bags the day before and was planning to drive to the airport and catch an early flight to Denver.

It was a busier than usual night at the ER, so she knew it was going to be the beginning of a long day attending the conference, but she had been looking forward to this event, especially with what she had endured during the COVID-19 pandemic.

As Serena walked to the door toward the parking lot, Susan, one of her favorite nurses whom she had known and worked with for the past three years, gave her a hug.

"Girl, you deserve this break – I hope you can rest and enjoy some time with your friends after what we've been through these past two years."

Serena couldn't agree more. As she got into her car, she took a deep breath, closed her eyes, and thought to herself, "A change of scenery, intellectual stimulation, and meeting up with some of my colleagues is just the medicine I need."

She was going to miss seeing her three pre-teenage children, but her husband of 14 years, Josh, was fully capable of managing in her absence and had an abundance of time on his hands.

As a former manager of a large national retail clothing chain, he had been laid off due to the pandemic. When the clothing chain filed for bankruptcy protection in the spring, and with the retail industry still reeling, Josh had not been able to find any meaningful employment. Instead, he was able to pick up the slack around the house and take care of the kids, driving them to and from their private school, allowing Serena to work night shifts that paid more than working day shifts. It was far from an ideal situation, but they made it work.

Benjamin, on the other hand, was a single man living in downtown Denver. He loved spending his free time rock climbing and reading books about personal finance and business.

Benjamin worked as a full-time physician at an urgent care group, owned by four physicians that had eight clinics throughout the Denver metropolitan area. Due to his proximity, he split his time working at four of the clinics.

His parents owned a successful dry-cleaning business in Denver, and Benjamin had become increasingly interested in learning more about how family businesses worked. He remembered how his parents had struggled in the early days in their business and later observed how their hard work and determination over the years began to pay off, growing a small marginally profitable dry cleaner into a profitable self-managed enterprise with 10 locations.

His parents now worked only 10 to 15 hours a week communicating directly with their leadership team. They enjoyed a comfortable lifestyle with an abundance of free time to travel. Ironically, one of their biggest concerns was wondering if, and when, the 34-year-old physician would get married. Not surprisingly, that was also becoming a concern of his girlfriend, Emily, of two years. He assured his parents that he would get married when he was good and ready, but that he enjoyed the freedom that he had at the present.

Benjamin was blessed with even more entrepreneurs in the family – an aunt and uncle who own a multi-office chiropractic clinic in Colorado. They started their career acquiring an existing chiropractic wellness center, then started hiring associates as their practice grew.

Their unique, holistic approach to healthcare allowed them to create a niche in the marketplace that resulted in extraordinary growth and expansion to six locations up and down Colorado's Front Range. Each time they opened a new clinic, they sold half of the clinic to the associate who worked in that clinic and continued to own the remaining half. They also purchased the land and facilities in which each clinic operated and leased the property back to the clinic.

Benjamin's interest in personal finance and business was partly due to being raised in a family of entrepreneurs, but he realized that he had never received any formal education in these areas during his medical training. Now that he was out on his own and making good money, he was concerned about how little he had left in his checking account each month.

He told his parents, "I remember when I was a resident, the thought of making $400,000 a year as a physician felt like winning the lottery. Now, it seems like the money goes out as fast as it comes in, and there is little left. I've become really good at spending money, but I really struggle at saving."

Indira had a different background growing up. Her parents immigrated from India to Chicago when Indira was three years old. Her parents acquired, with the financial assistance of family back in India, their first hotel when Indira was 10, and she and her older sister, Malavika (Mal), spent every evening and most of the weekend working at the hotel for her parents.

Four years later, her parents purchased a second hotel nearby. By the time Indira finished college, her parents owned 17 hotels throughout Chicagoland. When Indira and Mal came home from college every break, they worked with their parents. Her parents saved enough to put both of their daughters through college, as well as medical school for Indira and graduate business school, law school, and graduate tax law school for her sister. Mal even went on to pass the Certified Public Accountancy exam and bar exam.

After Indira completed her residency in emergency room medicine, she started her medical career working for one of the largest healthcare networks in Chicago at one of its hospitals located in North Shore. She and her husband of 13 years, Chatura, had a 12-and-a-half-year-old son and an 11-year-old daughter.

Meanwhile, Mal had recently joined the CPA firm that her parents had used for the past 24 years. Mal's father was so happy when she told him the news on the phone.

"You are going to love them! They have an incredible team and are very proactive with their tax and business clients. They have helped your mother and me save so much money in taxes. They are a big reason why we have been so successful financially," he said brightly.

As Mal pondered what her father had said, she eased herself down into her ergonomic chair in her office. She closed her eyes and leaned back smiling, thinking about how fortunate she was to have wise, hard-working parents and a work environment that had such an empowering culture and team members who loved what they did for a living.

Although Indira and Mal had very similar upbringing, their perspectives toward money were vastly different. Mal was born with her parents' frugality, but Indira was much more interested in enjoying the finer things in life like jewelry, a big home, and nice cars. She had recently purchased a condo at a popular ski resort in Colorado, which she hoped to be able to enjoy several times a year.

"I feel that I deferred the gratification of having nice things while I was completing my medical training; I am trying to make up for lost time. And I can't believe how much in taxes they take out of my paycheck!" Indira confided in her sister one time over coffee.

Malavika paused for a moment and said to her sister, "You might want to meet with the senior partner of the CPA firm I work for. Our firm focuses on tax planning for high-income professionals, entrepreneurs like mom and dad, and real estate investors. If you'd like me to, I would be happy to see if he is taking on any new clients and if he would be willing to meet with you."

Indira's face lit up as she exclaimed, "That would be great! I think I need help. I've been out of residency for almost five years, and I don't have much to show for it."

Elijah, Serena, Benjamin, and Indira were classmates at the University of Kansas School of Medicine. Although they had each come from different backgrounds and upbringings, they had become best friends in medical school and did almost everything together. Their admiration and affection for each other was palpable. In fact, they were so close their classmates called them, "The Motley Crew." On the surface, one wouldn't think they would be best of friends, but through all their differences, they found so much in common.

It had been 10 years since they graduated, each one heading off to different cities to start their residency programs. All of them chose emergency room medicine as their specialty. There was something about the adrenaline rush of working in an ER and not having to work on call that attracted them. Besides Benjamin being a groomsman in Elijah and Joy's wedding, the four had not seen each other in person since medical school, but they had stayed in touch with each other frequently by phone, social media, and email.

In their last email exchange, they all agreed to meet over dinner and drinks at the upcoming Rocky Mountain Trauma & Emergency Medicine Conference in Denver.

There were hundreds of attendees at the conference. Serena spotted Elijah immediately as she walked into the main conference hall. She waved and motioned to Elijah to save a seat for her.

Outside in the lobby, Benjamin and Indira saw each other in the registration sign-in line. Indira ran up to Benjamin and gave him a big hug. "Boy, it's been forever since I've seen you!" Indira exclaimed, tears welling up in her eyes.

Benjamin and Indira had formed a close bond in medical school. Since they were in most of the same classes and labs, they decided in their first year to form a study group with a few other students. Benjamin had a unique skill of taking incredibly detailed notes during class, and Indira was able to put the group's notes into a concise outline that helped each of them be well prepared for exams. They also enjoyed getting together in their spare time over coffee talking about what they planned to do after they completed their residency programs. Both of them had big dreams of owning their own business and real estate and retiring early from the practice of medicine.

That evening, the four former classmates jumped in an Uber to Maggiano's Little Italy.

"It has one of the best lasagnas anywhere – and their chicken marsala is to die for!" Benjamin shared enthusiastically as they were all cramped together in the sedan as it sped to the restaurant.

Serena smiled, "That sounds so good because I'm starving. I'm going on 20 hours living on caffeine and a protein bar!"

They all laughed out of empathy.

After being seated and making their menu selections, they settled down to enjoy a nice glass of wine.

"I'd like to make a toast!" Benjamin declared as he raised his glass of Salute Amico, one of Maggiano's best white wines.

"Here's to great friends who are each doing amazing things on the frontline of medicine during these times. To our health and our patients' health!" he said with a wide grin. There was a collective "Cheers!" as they each clinked their glasses and enjoyed the first sip.

Three hours flew by as the four doctors shared stories about their personal lives since residency, classmates that they stayed in touch with, and the stress and exhaustion of working during the past year and a half of the pandemic. The effects of a few glasses of wine and enjoying a wonderful Italian dinner began to sink in.

After a momentary pause and with a serious look on his face, Benjamin asked the group, "So what has been the biggest surprise that you have had over the past five years?"

"For me, it's the incredible experience of having four young children so close in age. I never realized how much work has been involved for Joy, especially with the long hours I work – and we even have the benefit of my parents helping out. I can't imagine how people do it with both spouses working!" said Elijah.

"It's not easy," Serena responded quickly, shaking her head. "It definitely takes a village. I remember when we had our third child after the twins, Josh and I laughed that we needed to go from playing one-on-one defense to playing zone defense," she continued.

They all chuckled.

Benjamin chimed in, "That's one of the reasons I haven't gotten married and started raising a family. I know that my days of enjoying my freedom are limited, so I'm trying to make the most of the things that I will need to sacrifice someday."

"You know," Elijah said, "the tremendous joy and happiness of having four wonderful children has definitely outweighed any cost or inconvenience."

Benjamin then said, "Not to take from children and family, I would have to say that the biggest surprise for me over the past five years is how little I have to show for all of the money I've made. When I was a resident, I remembered dreaming about how much money I was going to make and save when I started working full time as a physician."

The group nodded in agreement.

"I thought I'd have at least half a million dollars saved and be well on my way to being a multi-millionaire by this point in my life. At this pace, it may be closer to age 45 or 50. It certainly hasn't been the 'rainbows and butterflies' I thought it would be," he said quietly as he stared woefully at his empty wine glass.

Serena put her hand on Benjamin's shoulder consolingly, "That would have been true if you had continued to live like a struggling resident. The one thing I've learned is how tempting it is to buy things that

I think I also need. They all seem like smart decisions at the time."

Elijah nodded in agreement.

"It's like there is an irresistible urge to spend money when you have it. Joy and I don't penny-pinch when it comes to having nice clothes for our kids, taking fun vacations, and living in a big house. Everywhere I look, it's 'spend, spend, spend!'"

He paused, then continued, "I need a loud voice in my head to start shouting 'save, save, save!'"

The server poured another round of wine for the crew when Indira had a thought.

"I have an idea that may benefit all of us." The others looked at her with curiosity as she continued, "My sister, Mal, has been working at a CPA firm that works with clients like us. They focus on proactive tax, business, and financial advice. My parents are clients of the firm, and they swear that the advice they received over the years is a big reason why they have been so successful financially and with their business. Mal offered to introduce me to the senior partner. I have an appointment next week, and I'm hoping they are accepting new clients. If they are, I'd be happy to introduce him too..."

Elijah, Serena, and Benjamin interrupted her in unison, "We want in!"

"Okay!" Indira responded with a somewhat surprised look on her face. She didn't think that they would be excited about meeting an accountant, "I'll ask Mal to put in a good word and, hopefully, we can all meet together with him."

As the lovely evening full of rich conversation, good food, and wine ended, they walked out the door of the restaurant. Serena turned and said to the others, "I am so happy we were able to go to this conference and meet this evening to share what's been going on in our lives. I miss the times we had together in medical school and am so thankful to have good loyal friends like you!" as a tear began to form.

Benjamin added, "I haven't had friends that I have been closer to than you guys – I guess that's what happens when you spend so much time studying together in medical school."

They all embraced in a big group hug as they waited for the Uber to arrive.

Chapter 2

The Counselor

The Minister and the Monk

Two childhood friends grew up together and went their separate ways. One becomes a rich and powerful minister to a king, the other becomes a humble monk.

Several years later, they meet and catch up. The well-dressed and portly minister takes pity on the shabby and thin monk. Seeking to help, the minister says:

"You know, if you could learn to cater to the king, you wouldn't have to live on rice and beans." To which the monk responds: "If you could learn to live on rice and beans, you wouldn't have to cater to the king."

When the four doctors checked their emails the following morning, each of them had a Zoom meeting invitation with Will, the managing partner of Mal's CPA firm. They were impressed how quickly Mal was able to coordinate a meeting.

When everyone logged into the Zoom call the following week, Mal welcomed everyone and introduced William George to each of the doctors.

"Good morning, everyone. It is a pleasure to meet each of you virtually, and I appreciate you taking time out of your busy schedule this morning. By the way, I go by 'Will' to my family and friends, which I hope you will consider yourself a part of if you become a client," Will said warmly.

"I appreciate Mal's success at finding a time we were all available. Let's start with each of you sharing a little about your background and the journey that led you to this meeting today. Who would like to start?"

Indira volunteered to go first, saying, "Will, thank you for meeting with us today. Speaking for myself, I needed to meet with you several years ago when I started working as an emergency room physician. My parents have spoken very highly of you and believe that you are a big reason for their business and financial success."

Will chimed in, "Well, thank you for the kind words. I can certainly see the family resemblance between you, Mal, and your beautiful mother!"

Indira blushed, then continued, "I feel like I am a living version of 'Humpty Dumpty' after he had fallen off the wall and broke into pieces. I don't know how to put the pieces together again!"

The group laughed at her metaphor.

She continued, "I have been out of residency for almost five years, and I have not been able to get a handle on my personal finances. It is so difficult to save money. I feel that after taxes are withheld and I pay bills, there is very little left. Admittedly, I enjoy buying some of the nicer things in life for Chatura and my kids, but it seems like every time I think I'm going to have some money to save, I get a credit card statement in the mail that needs to be paid instead."

"I'm in the same boat as Indira. My biggest concern is how much tax I'm paying. It's by far my biggest expense, and I feel helpless in doing anything about it." Benjamin added. "I had big plans when I finished medical school and was confident that I was going to be a millionaire by 35. I'm single at the moment, but the thought of supporting a wife and children is scary. If I don't get my financial house in order before I get married and start a family, it would be like jumping from the frying pan into the fire in terms of added stress!"

"Amen to that!" Elijah interjected, "It has been financially tight for my wife, Joy, and four children. It doesn't seem like we should be having stress over our finances with my income. I definitely need help in getting on the right path."

Serena nodded and said, "My husband has been out of work since the pandemic, and it has been stressful for us too. I feel embarrassed and ashamed to seek help or ask for advice. On the one hand, I know an incredible amount about emergency medicine and treating patients, but on the other hand, I feel financially illiterate. Other than what our parents taught us, none of us received any financial or business teaching."

"Serena, none of you should feel embarrassed or ashamed about any lack of financial knowledge," Will responded. "Based on my experience, it is very common that doctors lack the tools and skills to adequately handle money. When a doctor has all this money dumped on them starting post-residency, they assume they will know how to make sound financial decisions. The good news is that each of you have been working for only a short period so far, so there is plenty of time to get on track."

Benjamin frowned. "With the pressure that all of us have been through being on the front line of medicine during the pandemic, and all of the regulation and bureaucracy we are subject to, I'm not sure I want to stay in medicine my whole career. I'm already burned out."

Each of the other doctors nodded their heads in agreement.

"I need help to put together a plan to create other sources of income, or possibly change careers," sighed Benjamin.

Will was a 60-year-old man. His white beard and graying hair, along with his 35 years as a CPA, reflected the vast wisdom and knowledge he had acquired in his career. In fact, his thirst for knowledge resulted in him getting his law degree and a graduate tax law degree in his twenties. He expanded his knowledge by obtaining his Personal Financial Specialist designation through the American Institute of CPAs and became a Certified Tax Specialist with the American Institute of Tax Planners.

"Like I mentioned, you are not alone in your knowledge of finances and not being where you want to be financially," answered Will. "Doctors have difficulty saving money for a number of reasons. First, unlike your classmates outside of the medical profession who started working right after college, you are getting a late start – 8 to 10 years later than your college friends. You've built up a lot of deferred gratification over the many years of medical training. Next, getting paid a big salary right after residency is kind of like winning the lottery, and we know what happens when someone wins the lottery – the money is spent within a couple of years. Third, there is pressure for doctors to look the part – drive a nice car, buy an expensive house, send your kids to private schools – you are tempted to 'keep up with the Joneses.' Fourth, you are a target of unscrupulous financial and investment advisors who want to take advantage of your income – once a financial advisor finds out you're a doctor, they come knocking at your door. Next, you've spent your life focused on helping your patients and their health, not learning about finance, business, and investing. Finally, learning good financial management and habits and how to evaluate business and investment risks is boring for most doctors – it's hard to be motivated and disciplined to learn what it takes to be financially successful."

"Wow," Elijah exclaimed, "I think I fit all of those reasons."

"Me, too!" added Serena.

"So, Will, if I could ask, how do we start learning about personal finance, starting a business, or making smart investments?" asked Benjamin.

"Benjamin, there is not a simple answer, it's personal to each person. Everyone looks for the 'silver bullet,' but it depends on your goals, knowing your strengths and weaknesses, and having the discipline, time, and willingness to learn. And probably the most important thing is to commit to a written plan that helps you stay focused on your goals and measure your progress along the way. The reason why we exist as a CPA firm is to help our clients become financially independent. Financial independence means different things to different people. Our job is to help you create clarity, focus, and a disciplined approach to reaching financial independence as soon as possible."

Indira unmuted her microphone and asked Will, "So, I have two questions – how do we get started? And are you able to help us?"

"Regarding your first question, just like your parents did 30 years ago, it starts with a plan and sticking with it. On the second question, it depends on whether you are the right fit for us and we are the right fit for you. We have had a lot of prospective clients come to us to have us solve their financial or business problems, but only a handful are willing to invest the time and effort to learn the skills and acquire the knowledge to be successful."

"We've developed a unique process to help our clients – it's called The Strategic Wealth System™," continued Will. "We start all of our new client relationships with a Strategic Blueprint. It allows us to learn about a person's goals, understand their challenges, and help them take advantage of the opportunities they have. Based on the information we collect, we create a personalized roadmap with tax, financial, and/or business strategies and recommendations. If we believe that we are a good fit for each other, then we start implementing the specific recommendations and strategies. One of the key aspects of The Strategic Wealth System™ is what we call the Quarterly Pulse. It happens every 90 days and allows us to make sure we are still on track with a client's goals, identify any challenges that need to be eliminated, opportunities to be captured, and update the plan with any new goals as the old goals are reached."

Benjamin asked, "How would I know if I'm a good fit and your firm is a good fit for me?"

"Great question," Will answered. "In determining whether we are a good fit for you, it depends on whether you believe we can meet your expectations. In evaluating whether you are a good fit, we have a set of strict rules that need to be met. However, we don't call them 'rules' per se. Instead, we call them 'Get Tos,' in that you "Get To" follow them. Plus, the word 'rule' does not sound very fun. Our goal is to help you be successful. It requires open and honest communication between us. A client needs to be open-minded, vulnerable, accountable, growth-oriented, and be willing to take risks. One of my favorite pieces of advice on risk comes from David Viscott in his book *Risking*. He wrote that 'If you cannot risk, you cannot grow. If you cannot grow, you cannot become your best. If you cannot become your best, you cannot be happy. If you cannot be happy, what else matters?'"

E	B
S	I

E is for Employee
S is for Self-Employed
B is for Business Owner
I is for Investor

"Just like a professional athlete or someone who is training for the Olympics, they have coaches who help them win. In a similar manner, we serve as a coach to our clients. Very few people can be successful without having help from the right coach or coaches. In our process, we teach lessons over a three- to five-year period to our clients. These lessons build a strong foundation that we can maintain and build on over the course of our relationship," Will added, then stated, "If at any time along the way either we or you do not believe we are a good fit, either one of us can terminate the relationship."

Will shared his screen and pulled up one of his most used presentations.

"We discovered while working with our clients, they typically fall into one of four categories. Robert Kiyosaki, in his book *Rich Dad's CASHFLOW® Quadrant*, described the four categories as follows:

Robert states that everyone resides in at least one of the four quadrants of the CASHFLOW® Quadrant, and a person's quadrant placement is determined by where their cash flow comes from. The right side of the quadrant is for individuals who receive their cash flow from business and investment interests they own. Employees and self-employed individuals reside on the left side. Each quadrant is different, and individuals within each one have common characteristics. At our firm, we have created tracks in The Strategic Wealth System™ for each of the quadrants that clients fit into."

Will clicked to the next slide in the presentation.

"The E-Track is for our doctor clients who are currently employees; they might describe themselves with the following: 'I am looking for a safe, secure job with good compensation and benefits.'"

Click.

"The S-Track is for those who are independent contractors, part time or full time, or sole practitioners; they might say something like, 'My rate is $250 per hour, and I work 12-hour shifts, approximately 14 shifts per month.'"

Click.

"The B-Track is for those who are partners or shareholders of a group practice or who own, or want to own, businesses; they might say something like, 'I'm looking for a CFO to help me grow my business.'"

Click.

"The I-Track is for those who own, or want to own, investments that provide passive sources of income; someone on the I-Track may say, 'My personal cash flow is based on an internal rate of return from my investments.'"

Security vs. Freedom

"A doctor can be in one or more tracks based on their situation and goals. The path and the strategies needed to achieve financial independence is different for each track," explained Will.

"Most doctors are trained in school to pursue either the E-Track or the S-Track, partly due to being in debt with student loans. They need the security and safety that comes from having a steady income as an employee or independent contractor. Having a lavish lifestyle and big mortgage only adds to their dependency on a fixed or predictable income stream. Some doctors are able to begin the transition to the B-Track or I-Track early in their career, either part time or full time, depending on their need for security, desire for freedom, and willingness to be educated in the B-Track or I-Track."

He continued, "Should we decide to work together, we will help you identify which quadrant you are in today, which quadrant you wish to move into, understand the differences, strengths and weaknesses of each one, and what strategies, personal education, and experience are needed to be financially successful in each of them."

"I see that our time is almost up. Do any of you have any more questions?" asked Will.

"Not me," replied Elijah.

"I don't," declared Serena.

"I'm sold – when can I get started?" asked Benjamin.

"Very good!" Will replied. "Starting is easy. Our New Client Success Manager, Angie, will send you an email with our Strategic Blueprint Starter Kit for you to complete and return. Our Client Services Manager, Lyndsay, will then send you an email with a link to a questionnaire for you to complete and a secure link to upload any important documents we may need to review. Once we receive the completed questionnaire and documents, Lyndsay will send you a link to schedule a 90-minute Zoom call to present and review the recommendations contained in your Strategic Blueprint. These calls will be with each of you since our recommendations will be tailored specifically to you. After we present our recommendations and provide you a quote to engage our services, you can decide if you would like to move forward. If you do, Lyndsay will schedule an Onboarding Meeting and our team will begin to implement the strategies and recommendations that you have chosen. Like I described earlier, every 90 days, we will check in on your Quarterly Pulse to make sure everything is being done and we are on track."

"Having a good structure and accountability are critical factors to having success. I have an idea that may be helpful in that regard – since you four are close friends and in a similar profession, I suggest that we meet as a group every five years to share our experiences and compare our results. In between those get-togethers, we will be working with each of you individually, of course," Will explained.

"That's wonderful! It sounds like a plan!" Indira exclaimed.

"I feel 10 pounds lighter! And who doesn't want that?" Elijah added, as the group nodded in agreement as the Zoom meeting came to an end.

Chapter 3
The Journey Begins

*"People overestimate what can be done in one year
and underestimate what can be done in ten."*
— Bill Gates

Step 1: Develop a Written Plan

Each doctor returned their Strategic Blueprint Starter Kit in less than a week. It took them another two weeks to complete the Strategic Blueprint questionnaire and upload their documents. They had scheduled a 90-minute Zoom call to discuss their strategies and recommendations.

Elijah and Joy scheduled their Zoom meeting first.

"Thank you for meeting today," Angie said pleasantly as they came online. "I hope all is well with you and your family since we last met."

The couple was equally pleased to see her. "Yes, we've been busy as usual and we are doing well, thank you for asking," Elijah replied.

After they had exchanged pleasantries, Angie told them Lyndsay and Will were also on the call.

She reminded them that the emails they received recently about their Strategic Blueprint questionnaire were from Lyndsay.

"Lyndsay is our Client Services Manager and will be leading the Onboarding Process if you decide to move forward after our call today," she said. She added that Will came up with the strategies and recommendations they were about to discuss.

"Hello," Lyndsay beamed.

Will waved at them. "Greetings."

Angie informed the couple that they'd learn the first lesson during the meeting. She said they would review their current situation and discuss their goals for the next five years. They would also identify any challenges they currently had. They would talk about their opportunities and explore the strengths that they could build on.

"We believe that developing a written plan, which we call your Strategic Blueprint, is the first step in the journey of helping our clients to achieve financial independence in their lives," she said. "Your Strategic Blueprint helps us focus on the things that are most important to you, prioritize the action items, and provide clarity, direction, and focus for us and our team."

She explained that it would also give the couple a roadmap so that they'd have better control and understanding of every action that they'd be taking.

She told them one saying everyone at the office liked. It was Benjamin Franklin's "If you fail to plan, you are planning to fail."

"Based on our experience, if we don't start with a written plan, it typically results in a lot of time spent merely putting out fires or solving short-term problems and failing to make progress with your goals," she told the couple.

Joy agreed. "That makes sense."

Following this, Angie revealed that the Strategic Blueprint was the first step the couple would take in order to build a long-term strategic plan to achieve their goals.

"Our clients who have a strategic plan that has both written goals and concrete plans, and is updated regularly, are far more successful at reaching their goals than those who do not have a plan," she pointed out.

"To emphasize this point, I always like to bring up a slide from a study," she said as she opened a slide.

Angie told Elijah and Joy that she had heard of several Harvard

MBA studies on goal setting. They analyzed graduating classes to determine how many had set goals and had a plan for their attainment.

In one such study, the graduating class was asked a single question about their goals in life:

"Have you set written goals and created a plan for their attainment?"

Prior to graduation, it was determined that:

- 84% of the entire class had set no goals at all.
- 13% of the class had set written goals but had no concrete plans.
- 3% of the class had both written goals and concrete plans."

"How do you think this turned out for these groups?" Angie asked her audience.

Elijah responded, "I imagine those with written goals and a concrete plan did better than those that didn't have them."

"You're right," Angie replied. "Ten years later, the 13% of the class that had set written goals but had not created plans were making twice as much money as the 84% of the class that had set no goals at all. The kicker, however, is that the 3% of the class that had both written goals and a plan were making 10 times as much as the rest of the 97% of the class."

The slide made way for another slide that contained results from a similar study, done by the Statistic Brain Research Institute. It examined how many people made New Year's resolutions and how many of them stuck with their goals.

This study reported that:

- 45% usually make goals
- 17% infrequently make goals
- 38% never make goals

Angie paused to let the results sink in before moving on to the next slide.

"Another interesting measure from this study was how far people got before they threw in the proverbial towel," she said.

- 75% of people made it through their first week
- 71% of people made it past two weeks

- 64% of people made it past one month
- 46% of people made it past six months

She asked the couple what they thought the results implied.

Joy answered this time. She said it meant that 25% of people who made New Year's goals and resolutions didn't even make it through their first week of the new year.

"Exactly," Angie agreed.

"Because of the difficulty people have setting and staying with their goals and plans, that is why we emphasize the importance of planning to our clients and include it in our process," she explained.

She then transitioned to a new part of the presentation on The Strategic Wealth System™. The slides outlined the key requirements a relationship seeking financial independence would need.

She asked the couple to study the requirements and get onboard with this type of goal setting.

- **The goals must be highly specific and measurable.** Instead of saying, "You want to be rich," come up with an exact amount of net worth you want to have by a specific time.

- **There must be strong reasons to achieve the goals.** If you have a strong, motivating reason to achieve a goal, you'll follow through – if you don't, you'll quit.

- **The plan must be thoroughly documented so that the goals have direction.** Describe how you are going to achieve these goals by creating a roadmap of action steps that will take you from Point A to Point B.

- **The goals must be managed, tracked, and adjusted regularly.** For example, if you set the goal of saving $100,000 in 12 months, you can come up with monthly and weekly goals to achieve the larger goal. It's important to break the bigger goal into smaller goals, i.e., baby steps. When you try to do everything at once, progress can be very slow.

Next, she asked the couple if they'd seen *What About Bob*, a movie starring Bill Murray.

"We love that movie – it's so funny!" Joy remembered.

Angie said she loved it too. She decided to make a point with a part of the story.

"As you remember, Bob is the crazy guy who drives his psychiatrist crazy," she said. "The psychiatrist had written a book called Baby Steps. The statement 'You can get anywhere if you simply go one step at a time' is the framework of the movie. We use 'baby steps' to walk through The Strategic Wealth System™."

It got through to Elijah.

"I now understand why we haven't made as much progress financially over the past five years," he said. "We didn't know what we didn't know. We had no plan at all. We just spent money on things that we needed or wanted at the time. I now understand the importance of having a written plan with specific goals…"

"And a method of tracking and updating it regularly by taking baby steps," Joy added on cue.

The couple wanted to be on the E-Track.

It was clear that Elijah needed job security. Raising a family on only one income led him to believe that risks weren't a great option.

Angie, sensing that Elijah wasn't totally content with the E-Track, piped in, "You know, our clients go through different seasons of life where different tracks are attractive. There's nothing to say that moving to the S-, B- or I-Track can't happen later. Maybe we can talk more about that."

A few days later Serena had her 90-minute Zoom meeting with Angie and others.

She was enthusiastic.

"Elijah called me after his meeting with you," she told Angie. "He and Joy are so excited about starting to work on their goals. I'm really looking forward to what kind of plan we come up with today!"

"Thank you," Angie replied, "We are looking forward to showing how we can help you as well."

She shared the first lesson with Serena just like she did with Joy and Elijah.

After they had agreed on the importance of having a written plan with specific goals and action steps, she jumped into the second lesson.

It was: "Make your future bigger than your past."

"At first glance, this lesson may not seem that important, but let me explain why it is," Angie started.

"Most people begin thinking about their future goals and what they want to achieve during their lifetimes. As we've observed, most of them lose focus and discipline and get frustrated when they don't reach their goals."

"Henry David Thoreau once said, 'Most men lead lives of quiet desperation.' Most people live their lives and never reach their potential. They have a mindset that if they think they can't, they won't; if they think they can, there's a good chance they will."

She supported her point with a bible passage. "Proverbs 23:7 says, 'For as he thinks within himself, so he is.'"

"The secret of living an exceptional life starts with thinking thoughts of an exceptional life. That is where it is important to have a mindset of making your future bigger than your past," she revealed. "More than ever, this is more important for doctors to have this mindset with the increasing stress – especially those on the frontline during the pandemic, and professional burnout facing them."

Serena interrupted her at this point. "I can so identify with the burnout," she said. "It makes it difficult to get excited about the future if it continues at this hectic pace."

Angie nodded. "Having a picture of a bigger future brings greater focus, confidence, learning, opportunities, and quality of life," she pointed out.

"Some people's bigger futures are about themselves, and others include contributions to other people. Our experiences in the past are important to learn from because they can become the raw material for creating an even bigger future."

"Having this attitude of the past gives us an insatiable desire for even more enjoyable and better experiences," she said.

Angie opened up a slide. She said the Strategic Blueprint questionnaire helped their clients think about a bigger future with four questions:

Question 1: *If we were having this discussion five years from today, and you were looking back over those three years, what has to happen in your life, both personally and professionally, for you to feel happy with your progress?*

Question 2: *Specifically, what dangers or challenges do you have now that need to be eliminated?*

Question 3: *What are the biggest opportunities you have now that need to be captured?*

Question 4: *What strengths do you have that need to be maximized?*

Serena had written a clear response to the first question.

"In the next five years, save $250,000 in retirement or other investments, set aside $25,000 for my children's college education," she'd said. "I would also like to find out how I can reduce my taxes. Professionally, I would like to explore other work opportunities where I can make more money, possibly as an independent contractor."

Benjamin's answer was similar.

"Personally, I would like to save $100,000 each year in retirement accounts and potentially get married in the next five years," he'd written. "Professionally, I have always dreamed of owning a business, such as a clinic or several clinics; so, I'd like to have started or bought my first business and restructured my current employment relationship to make more money."

Indira also had specific goals.

"I would like to fund my retirement plan with at least $50,000 each year and save up enough money to purchase some rental property. Also, I would like to buy or start my own medical-related business."

Elijah was a family man, so his numbers were bigger.

"Personally, I would like to have contributed $200,000 to my retirement account, saved another $100,000 in other investments, set up and funded college savings accounts for each of my children with at least $20,000 in each, paid off my student loans of $110,000," he'd written. "Professionally, I would like to be able to pick up an extra two or three shifts each month at the hospital to be able to fund the savings and pay off the debt listed above."

Elijah made all of his $400,000 income from the hospital where he works. This was the key reason he fell into the CASHFLOW® Quadrant's "E" (for employee) quadrant.

After some thought, he said he wanted to be in a different quadrant. He estimated that he could earn an additional $50,000 to $75,000 every year by working additional shifts at other hospitals and clinics.

So, the group explored if he could do that as a Form 1099 independent contractor and discussed the pros and cons of 1099 income versus W-2 income.

They concluded, after a thorough discussion, to create a professional entity that will make the 1099 income. They also discussed strategies to eliminate obstacles, capture current opportunities and maximize his strengths.

The firm was able to lower the couple's annual income tax liability by $24,500 per year. They also created a tax and financial roadmap to help them achieve their financial goals in five years. And finally, they gave the duo tools that they could use to manage their cash flow and monitor their progress.

"Both of my parents had been employees for large organizations their entire career," he said. "My father, employed as a tenured college professor and mother, employed by a state government agency, both with secure pensions, thought owning a business, with the ups and downs that they have, was too risky."

He said they had always advised him to go the safe and secure route which was to find a job with a hospital after his residency.

Will chimed in, "It's not uncommon for prospective clients and clients to not know that there can be other ways to financial independence. I'm excited to see where this takes you."

Each of the four doctors described, for the most part, the different challenges that they were facing. They said they were frustrated they weren't in a better place financially. Plus, they were paying too much in taxes.

They all had similar opportunities and strengths. They wanted to learn how they could save and invest better, and they were intelligent enough to learn new things.

Step 2: Reduce Taxes

Why Are Taxes So Complicated?

Benjamin took it upon himself to fly in for a session with Will on reducing his taxes. Seeing so much of his income leave through tax had always been a tough pill to swallow. Will started the next session with Benjamin with a quote.

"Albert Einstein once said, 'The hardest thing in the world to understand is the income tax,'" he stated, matter-of-factly.

He pointed out that Einstein died in 1955, and at that time, The Internal Revenue Code of 1954 was only 907 pages. But currently, the Code has a total of 2,652 pages. At approximately 450 words per page, that puts the Code at well over 1 million words.

He said, by comparison, the King James Version of the Bible has 788,280 words, *War and Peace* has 560,000 words, and the *Harry Potter* series is just over 1 million words.

"If you add in the Department of Treasury Regulations, IRS Revenue Rulings, and other pronouncements and clarifications, which with the Code make up the tax law, it puts the estimated total number of current pages at over 70,000 and ever-increasing, as this graph shows," he said, pointing to a graph.

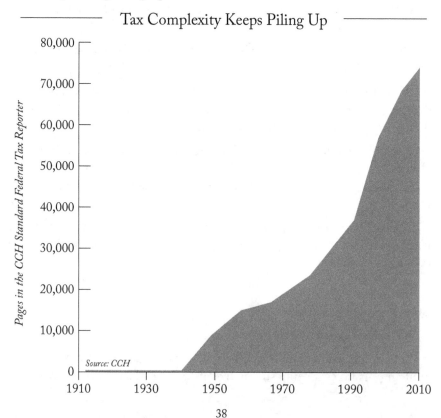

Tax Complexity Keeps Piling Up

Pages in the CCH Standard Federal Tax Reporter

Source: CCH

"There is little doubt in anyone's mind today that the tax code has become one of the most difficult things to understand, and it is very unlikely that the tax code will become simplified anytime soon," he said.

Benjamin was curious. "Why are taxes so complicated?"

Will told him the question doesn't have an easy answer.

"Our tax system could be simple if its only purpose were to raise revenue," he said. "But it has other goals, including fairness, efficiency, and enforceability. And Congress has used the tax system to influence social policy, as well as to deliver benefits for specific groups and industries."

Will stopped to take a sip of coffee before he continued.

"Notwithstanding its complexity, most of the tax law is written to people in the 'B' and 'I' quadrants, but some tax benefits apply to the 'S' quadrant too. Our tax system is a stimulus package to business owners and investors. Congress passes tax legislation to incentivize certain behavior and actions from taxpayers."

"I think it's important to understand the grander picture of income taxes and their future," he said as he pulled up a new slide posing a question.

Will Taxes Likely Increase in the Future?

Yes, because of:

- Social Security
- Medicare
- National Debt

"There are several reasons why taxes will increase again in the future," he revealed. "The three biggest reasons are due to the expected increase in costs for Social Security, Medicare, and National Debt."

"Consider also that there are other costs likely to require the government to need more revenue, including defense, welfare, healthcare, and infrastructure needs."

Will made sure Benjamin was still paying attention.

"I think it's great to understand the context. Let's examine the three biggest causes for future tax increases," he said as he transitioned to the next slide.

Social Security

"When we look at the history of our Social Security, which was enacted in 1935, there were 42 workers who paid Social Security taxes for every single beneficiary of Social Security retirement income beginning at the age of 65," he said.

"Ironically, the life expectancy of a beneficiary was only 62 at the time. As of 2018, there were fewer than 3 workers for every 1 beneficiary. Ten years from now, it is expected that there will be only 2 workers for every 1 beneficiary."

"Unless Social Security taxes increase, it is likely that Social Security benefits will be restricted based on an individual's income needs. Since so many retirees are dependent on it as a source of income, it is likely that it will remain but will increase the tax burden paid by workers."

Medicare Tax

"Adding to the shifting demographics of workers and beneficiaries, the Medicare Trust Fund, which was $200.4B in 2018, is expected to be a negative $50.5B in 2026, as the graph illustrates," he said.

From the 2019 Medicare Trustee Report (in billions)				
Year	Income	Expenses	Change in Fund	Fund at Year End
2018	$306.6	$308.2	-$1.6	$200.4
2019	$323.7	$330.4	-$6.7	$193.7
2020	$341.9	$351.8	-$9.9	$183.8
2021	$360.2	$375.8	-$15.7	$168.1
2022	$378.2	$403.5	-$24.6	$143.5
2023	$398.2	$432.6	-$34.5	$109.0
2024	$418.7	$462.5	-$43.8	$65.3
2025	$439.5	$494.2	-$54.6	$10.6
2026	$465.7	$526.9	-$61.2	-$50.5

"Medicare is also facing increasing costs of medical services and the fact that over 50% of baby boomers have yet to retire to be eligible for Medicare coverage," he added.

National Debt

He also said the country's National Debt was probably the biggest reason for future tax increases. He pulled up a graph of the U.S.' current Debt Clock (which is available in real time at www.usdebtclock.org):

From US Debt Clock.org

$30,023,495,550,402

Recorded from usdebtclock.org on Feb. 10, 2022

Will interjected, "Let's transition and look at how the government receives revenue through taxes."

How Is Income Taxed & Which Is Most Desirable?

Will said they'd need to get more information about income tax in order to understand the tax system. And that there were eleven types of income, according to the tax code.

- **Wages:** This is what one receives as an employee.
- **Profits or self-employment income:** This is what one makes in a business as sole proprietorship, partnership, or as an independent contractor.
- **S Corporation net income:** This is what one makes in a business that generates net income.
- **Rents:** This is what one gets paid from someone else who uses one's assets.
- **Royalties:** This is money earned from intellectual property.
- **Dividends:** This is payments received from a corporation that is part of its profits. Dividends are either ordinary or qualified.
- **Interest:** This is money one makes off the principal on a loan payable to one.

- **Short-term capital gain:** This is the net profit one makes from the sale of an asset owned for less than 1 year.

- **Long-term capital gain:** This is the net profit one makes from the sale of an asset owned for one year or longer.

- **Tax-Deferred Income:** This is income or gains that are in a pre-tax retirement account, such as a traditional IRA, 401(k), or profit-sharing plan.

- **Tax-Free Income:** This is income or gains that are in a post-tax retirement account, such as a Roth IRA or Roth 401(k), or a permanent life insurance policy.

Will explained that the tax law doesn't view these income types the same.

"This is an important concept to understand in achieving financial independence in the most tax-efficient way," he said.

He suggested viewing these income types as falling into one of three buckets, from least desirable to most desirable.

Least Desirable	More Desirable	Most Desirable

Wages (W-2 Income), Self-Employment Income	Rents, Royalties, Interest, Ordinary Dividends, Tax-Deferred Income, Short-Term Capital Gains, S-Corporation Income	Qualified Dividends, Long-Term Capital Gains, IRC §1202 Gain, Tax-Free Income

Then, Will explained the content of each bucket to Benjamin.

Least Desirable

Wages, or W-2 income, take the biggest hit under the U.S. tax system.

If one gets a W-2 income, they'll get hit with a FICA tax of 12.4%. One pays half and one's employer pays the other half up to the taxable wage base. It's the same with the Medicare tax of 2.9%.

Self-employment income is taxed in a similar manner, except that one pays the entire 12.4% self-employment tax on self-employment net income up to the FICA wage base and 2.9% on all self-employment net income.

Self-employment income is typically subject to a higher risk of an IRS audit than W-2 income, Will said.

"The only mitigating factor with self-employment tax is the ability to deduct one-half of the tax on your income tax return and the ability to claim business-related income tax deductions," Will said.

More Desirable

Rents, royalties, interest, short-term capital gain, S Corporation net income, and tax-deferred income are better when compared with W-2 income because one doesn't pay FICA or Medicare taxes with them, Will stated.

Royalties, interest, ordinary dividends, short-term capital gains, S Corporation net income, and distributions of tax-deferred income are taxed at your ordinary income tax bracket.

"So, while they are better than W-2 or self-employment income, they are not great. Because you're still paying tax on them at your highest marginal tax bracket," Will added.

Most Desirable

Will said qualified dividends and long-term capital gains are subject to tax at either 0%, 15%, or 20%, depending on one's marginal income tax bracket.

Will clicked to the next table.

"If you're in the highest marginal income tax bracket, which is 37%, your highest tax rate on qualified dividends and long-term capital gains is 20%."

"If you're in the 12% or lower marginal income tax bracket, your highest tax rate is 0% on qualified dividends and long-term capital gain."

"In between the 12% and 37% marginal income tax bracket, the tax rate is 15% on qualified dividends and long-term capital gain."

He said Section 1202 again applies when certain small business stock is sold. It provides an incentive for individual taxpayers to invest in small businesses. The amount of gain that can be excluded from tax is up to $10 million.

"Lastly, the best type of income is tax-free, which includes qualified distributions from Roth IRAs and Roth 401(k), and amounts borrowed against the cash surrender value of permanent life insurance," he said.

How Can I Protect My Retirement Savings From Taxes?

To answer this question, Will referred to *Power of Zero,* a book by David McKnight.

In it, the author lays out a three-bucket strategy for wealth accumulation that should be utilized by everyone and makes a case for why each bucket is necessary.

He said when one is building income to become financially independent someday, it is better to focus on building an equal amount of assets that generate income in these three buckets:

——————— Retirement Savings Buckets ———————

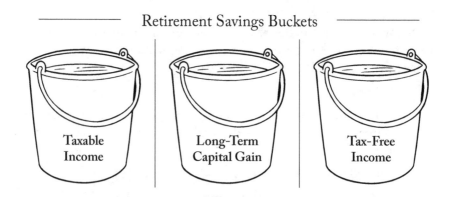

| Taxable | Long-Term | Tax-Free |
| Income | Capital Gain | Income |

He said the more Benjamin could accumulate in the long-term capital gain and tax-free income bucket, the better from a future taxable income standpoint.

"When you have assets that are allocated between the taxable, long-term capital gain, and tax-free buckets, you are better able to control and reduce your taxable income during retirement," he said. "The lower the amount of taxable income needed in order to provide for your retirement lifestyle needs, the lower the amount of assets needed."

He brought out several examples to explain further.

Example 1:

"Let's assume you would like to have $200,000 after-tax income during retirement. If 100% of your income is taxable at ordinary income, after paying tax at a 35% ordinary income tax rate, you would need to receive $307,692 in order to net $200,000 after paying $107,692 in income taxes," he said.

"If one applies the 4% Rule (meaning one's retirement income is 4% of one's retirement assets), one would need $7,692,300 in pre-ordinary tax income-producing assets to provide $200,000 in after-tax income in this example," he said.

Example 2:

"Assuming the same $200,000 after-tax income, if 50% of your after-tax income is ordinary income and 50% are proceeds from the sale of assets subject to long-term capital gain tax (assuming the gain represented half of the sale proceeds), you would need to receive $153,846 in fully taxable income plus $111,111 in sales proceeds, or a total of $264,957," he said, bringing up a table of numbers.

Example 2	
Taxable Income	$153,846
Less Ordinary Income Taxes	($53,846)
Net After-Tax Ordinary Income	$100,000
Sale Proceeds from Sale of Capital Asset	$111,111
Less Capital Gains Tax at 20% on 50% Gain	($11,111)
Net After-Tax Sales Proceeds	$100,000
Total After-Tax Income	$200,000

"Applying the 4% Rule, you would need $3,846,150 in pre-ordinary tax income-producing assets, plus $2,777,775 in long-term capital gain assets, or total assets of $6,623,925 to provide $200,000 in after-tax income in this example."

Example 3:

Assuming the same $200,000 after-tax income, Will said if 1/3 of one's after-tax income is ordinary income, 1/3 is capital gain (assuming the gain is 50% of the sale proceeds), and 1/3 is tax-free income, one would need to receive $102,564 in fully taxable income, $74,074 in sales proceeds, and $66,666 in tax-free income, or a total of $243,304.

Example 3	
Taxable Income	$102,564
Less Ordinary Income Taxes	($35,897)
Net After-Tax Ordinary Income	$66,667
Sale Proceeds from Sale of Capital Asset	$74,074
Less Capital Gains Tax at 20% on 50% Gain	($7,407)
Net After-Tax Sales Proceeds	$66,667
Tax-Free Income	$66,666
Total After-Tax Income	$200,000

"Applying the 4% Rule, you would need $2,564,100 in pre-ordinary tax income-producing assets, plus $1,851,850 in long-term capital gain assets, plus $1,666,650 in tax-free assets, or total assets of $6,082,600 to provide $200,000 in after-tax income," he said.

Example 4:

"Lastly, assuming the same $200,000, if 50% of your after-tax income is 50% from the sale of assets subject to long-term capital gains tax (assuming 50% of the sale proceeds are gain) and 50% from tax-free income, you would need to receive $111,111 in sales proceeds plus $100,000 in tax-free income, or a total of $211,111," Will said.

Example 4	
Sale Proceeds from Sale of Capital Asset	$111,111
Less Capital Gains Tax at 20% on 50% Gain	($11,111)
Net After-Tax Sales Proceeds	$100,000
Tax-Free Income	$100,000
Total After-Tax Income	$200,000

Comparing the 4 Examples			
Example	After-Tax Income Allocation	Total Income Needed	Total Assets Needed with 4% Rule
1	100% Ordinary Income	$307,692	$7,692,300
2	50% Ordinary Income and 50% Long-Term Capital Gains	$264,957	$6,623,925
3	33.3% Ordinary Income, 33.3% Long-Term Capital Gains, and 33.3% Tax-Free Income	$243,304	$6,082,600
4	50% Long-Term Capital Gains and 50% Tax-Free Income	$211,111	$5,277,775

"Applying the 4% Rule, you would need $2,777,775 in long-term capital gain assets, plus $2,500,000 in tax-free assets, or total assets of $5,277,775 to provide $200,000 in after-tax income in this example," he said.

Benjamin smiled. "Comparing the four examples, it is clear that the more tax-free and long-term capital gain income, and the less ordinary income, you receive, the less total assets you need to generate the same after-tax $200,000," he said.

Will told him he was correct.

"Accumulating a net worth of income-producing assets between $5,277,775 and $7,692,300 for retirement, depending on the tax treatment of the income and applying the 4% Rule, is unattainable for most doctors," he said. "Only those who start early in their career, have a high-income specialty, keep their lifestyle to a minimum, maximize their savings, and/or invest in successful businesses, real estate, or other ventures have a chance at accumulating enough to live on only 4% during retirement."

He said although the 4% Rule is certainly not required at this time, it does provide at least an ideal standard to ensure there is a likelihood of not running out of money during retirement.

He added that the discussion was to illustrate how much someone needed to accumulate in a tax-efficient manner in order to become financially independent.

"That's an incredible amount of money to need for retirement – even at only 35 years of age, I don't know if I can do it," Benjamin said, discouraged.

"I understand," Will responded empathetically. "The main purpose of this exercise is to realize that one needs to be very intentional, disciplined, and strategic if they wish to be financially independent during their lifetime."

He said with proper planning, the right strategies, and starting early, most doctors would be able to accumulate this amount.

"Now that we have discussed how taxes affect our income both during our working years and during our retirement years, I would like to discuss the importance of tax planning and taking advantage of allowable deductions and credits under our tax laws," Will said.

Benjamin's mood lifted. "Good!" he exclaimed. "I'm a little depressed after discussing the retirement struggles."

"Understood," replied Will, "but I can assure you that this next discussion will be more interesting."

He started by sharing a famous quote about tax planning.

He said Judge Learned Hand once wrote, "Any one may so arrange his affairs so that his taxes shall be as low as possible; he is not bound to choose that pattern which will best pay the Treasury; there is not even a patriotic duty to increase one's taxes."

"In our experience, one of the fastest ways that we can help put money into our client's pocket is to reduce their taxes," he stated.

"Unfortunately, many of our clients have had accountants who prepared their tax returns but never offered any tax planning ideas that could save them money. So many of these accountants are afraid of the tax law, so they don't learn how to take advantage of the law for their clients," he said.

According to him, some of them are also more interested in protecting themselves than reducing their client's tax liability.

"If you ask them about a particular legal tax strategy, if they are not properly educated, they often respond that it is either not legal or too risky. We refer to these types of accountants as 'Dr. No'," he explained.

Benjamin chuckled, "Yes, my parents have warned me about these types of accountants. They have always believed that the tax code is set up to reduce our tax burden legally."

"That's true," Will replied. "And it's also true that business owners and investors have the most tax breaks, so it is all the more important that they have a good tax advisor who knows the tax law."

He told Benjamin he'd met separately with Elijah, Serena, and Indira, to discuss and analyze each of their long-term goals, cash flow and net worth situations, and tax planning recommendations.

"Because both you and Indira have both expressed your interest in starting your own businesses, like each of your parents, I have asked Indira to join us in the next part of our discussion regarding tax and business planning," he said.

It sounded good to Benjamin. "Great!" he exclaimed.

"Indira and her sister, Mal, are waiting in the conference room for us," Will stated.

The two women were sitting at the conference room table when Will and Benjamin entered, and Benjamin walked up to Indira and gave her a hug. Then he hugged Mal who was standing next to her.

"It's great to see both of you again!" he exclaimed.

"It's wonderful to see you too!" Indira and Mal chorused.

Will told them to help themselves to any of the refreshments on the table.

"As I have discussed with each of you," he continued, "you have expressed an interest in someday starting your own clinic and becoming business owners like both of your parents."

"Yes," replied Indira with excitement, "growing up with entrepreneurial parents has given me great role models and mentors to learn about business and investing. I want to pursue my dream of owning my own clinic or clinics within the next year, and I need help with coming up with a financial and business plan. Since Mal and I have grown up as sisters, and I greatly appreciate her advice, I asked her to join me today."

Will liked the idea. "Excellent," he said, "The more mentors and advisors you have to guide you the better!"

He said the first topic he would like to address is the right business structure and his tax planning recommendations.

"You both shared with me that your current employers are willing to convert you from being W-2 employees to independent contractors and compensate you at your current salary and the cost of your employee benefits," he stated.

He then turned to a slide with five bullet points and spent the next hour explaining to Benjamin and Indira several important business and tax planning concepts.

- The various choices of business entities, including the pros/cons of each.
- The list of possible business-related deductions and reimbursable expenses.
- The types of business retirement plans and cost/benefits of each.
- Advanced tax, business, and financial planning strategies as the business grows over time.
- The importance of good record-keeping and accounting, including how to audit-proof your tax returns.

"In summary, we have several initial business and tax recommendations to be considered now," he explained.

	Initial Business and Tax Planning Recommendations for Indira and Benjamin
1	Establish a professional limited liability company ("PLLC") with the Secretary of State and file an election with the IRS to be taxed as an S corporation.
2	Set up an accountable expense reimbursement plan, and identify all your business-related expenses that are allowable income tax deductions for your PLLC.
3	Set up a bank account, and link it with a QuickBooks Online account, and set up a payroll account/provider for the PLLC.
4	Adopt a Lease Agreement between you and your PLLC to rent your home to up to 14 days each year for business purposes
5	Adopt a combination of the following retirement plans for your PLLC: 401(k), profit-sharing, defined benefit, and restricted property trust.
6	Conduct an annual independent reasonable compensation study to set your W-2 salary to be paid by the PLLC to you.

He brought up a diagram of how their PLLC looks with the arrows indicating how cash flows.

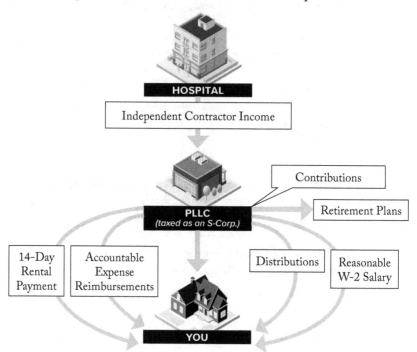

He said the best news was the annual tax savings that these recommendations would generate.

"Assuming you contribute between $50,000 and $75,000 to your retirement plans, you will save net taxes, after the cost of setting up and maintaining these recommendations, between $45,000 and $55,000 each year," he said enthusiastically.

Benjamin shouted. "Wow! That is almost the amount of money that I could contribute to the retirement plan every year!" he explained. "Rather than paying it in taxes, I'm adding it to my savings and net worth."

"Exactly," Will nodded in agreement.

He clicked his mouse for the next slide and continued, "When you are ready to start your clinic, and as it grows, we have additional recommendations to consider."

Next, he explained several additional business and advanced tax planning strategies available when the group start and grow their clinics.

He listed a couple of the more advanced business and tax planning strategies that would be available when they start.

	Additional Business and Tax Planning Recommendations for Indira and Benjamin
1	Form a separate limited liability company ("Clinic LLC") for each clinic with the Secretary of State.
2	Form an additional layer of asset protection, establish an additional LLC ("Clinic Holdings LLC") to own each of the Clinic LLCs, file an election for Holdings LLC to be taxed as an S corporation and each Clinic LLC to be taxed as a qualified S corporation subsidiary.
3	Establish a separate LLC ("Administrative Services LLC") to provide administrative services to the Holdings LLC pursuant to an Administrative Services Agreement to be taxed as a C corporation; adopt various fringe benefit plans to provide additional fringe benefits to you and your Clinic employees.
4	As your Clinics become successful, consider self-insuring a portion of your business risk by establishing a closely held insurance company ("CHIC")

He then said there were dozens of other strategies they could examine when the time comes.

He showed them a diagram of how the recommendations listed above relate to each other and the cash flow between the entities looks:

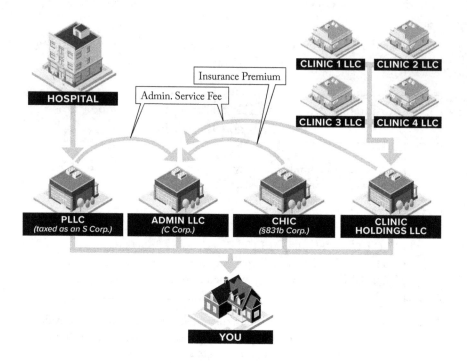

"To top it off, these additional strategies can save you tens of thousands of dollars in taxes," he explained.

"Very impressive," Indira exclaimed. She edged to the front of her seat.

"And for you, Indira," Will said. "Since you expressed interest in buying the land and building the office for each clinic, your tax savings will be even more."

He explained the tax and long-term financial benefits of owning and leasing the commercial real estate back to the clinics.

"You'll basically get to lease the real estate from the business, pay off the mortgage with tax-deductible dollars, and be able to defer, and possibly eliminate, any tax on gains when you sell the real estate. If structured properly, real estate is one of the best tax shelters and wealth creation strategies available."

"That's what my parents have always said," Indira responded, nodding her head in agreement.

The group spent the last 30 minutes reviewing the tax and financial projections in each of their Strategic Blueprints, the CPA firm's terms of services to be provided, and discussed the next steps to start implementing the recommendations.

"Thank you so much for including me in the meeting today. It was one of the most productive, educational, and rewarding meetings I have ever had." Indira exclaimed. She hugged the others as she walked out of the conference room.

Since he was in town, Benjamin remained behind for a whole new lesson on making the most of investments with his newfound tax savings.

Step 3: Control Cash Flow

Will started the meeting with Benjamin by telling him they were going to discuss cash flow. He described cash flow as most doctors' biggest challenge early on in their careers.

He said the first lesson about cash flow for Benjamin to learn was a quote by Robert Kiyosaki in *Rich Dad Poor Dad*.

"It's not how much money you make, but how much money you keep."

He told Benjamin it was Kiyosaki's definition of "financial intelligence."

"Financial intelligence is needed in order to see how money is flowing," he said. "Having financial intelligence allows a person to learn how money works and flows."

He explained that most professionals, especially doctors, focus on their professional education but neglect their financial education.

"Doctors have learned how to make money but not necessarily how to manage it. Professionals can be very intelligent and still be financially illiterate. They learned how to work hard for money but not how to make money work hard for them," he said.

He said financial intelligence starts with understanding one's Personal Cash Flow Statement and Net Worth Statement. That it's not just about the numbers but the story they tell and how they show where the money is flowing.

According to him, this understanding allows one to better control their cash flow. They will be able to make appropriate changes in how they spend and save money. And they will be able to focus on building their net worth.

He added that most people don't have the courage to make the necessary changes to be financially independent because change is painful.

"If you keep doing the same things, you will keep getting the same results. You are where you are today financially as a result of the financial decisions you have made up to this point," he said.

"If you like where you are, then keep it up," he continued. "Obviously, since you are meeting with me, it is clear you do not like where you are today. By choosing to be intentional and pursue financial independence, it helps you break through the temptation to remain doing the same things. You'll opt for the pain of change over the pain of staying where you are today."

Then Will enquired about Benjamin's understanding of his Personal Cash Flow Statement.

He asked about one of the homework assignments he was given months ago. It was to track his income and expenses over those months. They used it to create a Personal Cash Flow Statement.

"I did my best to list my monthly income and expenses, which I've been tracking over the past three months, but some of the expense amounts are estimates," Benjamin replied.

Benjamin's Personal Cash Flow Statement	
Income:	
Gross Annual Salary	$33,333
Interest Income	$31
Dividend Income	$198
Total Income	**$33,562**
Expenses:	
Taxes:	
FICA/Medicare Tax	$1,221
Federal Income Tax	$8,925
State Income Tax	$1,575
Total Taxes	**$11,721**
Mortgage	$3,512
Condo Association Dues	$35
Utilities	$1,105
Telephone	$218
Automobile Loan	$738
Student Loan	$1,457
Gas & Repairs	$727
Groceries/Food	$1,674
Insurance:	
Automobile	$346
Disability	$165
Life	$86
Total Insurance	**$597**
401(k) Deferral	$1,625
Medical/Dental Expense	$123
Furniture/Household	$1,620
Gym Membership	$90
Recreation/Entertainment	$4,941
Miscellaneous	$850
Total Expenses	**$30,037**
Net Cash Flow Surplus	**$3,525**

Will was happy with what he did.

"Excellent!" he exclaimed. "You did a great job of listing out in detail your expenses!"

"Thanks," Benjamin replied, adding that it wasn't easy.

"It took me several hours of going through my bank statements and credit card statements, and then putting them on a spreadsheet. I haven't been tracking my expenses like I probably should," he said.

Will explained that one of the reasons he was asked to track his income and expenses was to see if there was anything he'd need to address, like expenses that are excessive or unnecessary.

"If we don't track the numbers, it is difficult to identify problem areas. In your case, you are doing a good job of contributing the maximum amount to your 401(k), IRA, and Health Savings Account," he said.

He observed that Benjamin's net surplus amount was somewhat low for someone in his position.

"Depending on how much savings you have accumulated, you may want to cut back on some of your discretionary expenses so that you have a larger cash reserve to be able to start the business that you mentioned as one of your goals," he advised.

Benjamin agreed. "I think my recreation and entertainment expenses are excessive," he explained.

"Living in Colorado, I spend a lot of my free time up in the mountains with my friends, skiing in the winter and biking in the summer. Those are expensive activities, and I may be a little out of control," he said, somewhat embarrassed.

Will told him he had no reason to be ashamed.

"You are in a season of your life, being young and healthy, that you can and should enjoy all of those activities, and what better place than in beautiful Colorado!" he said.

Then he asked Benjamin if he gained any insights from the Cash Flow exercise.

Benjamin did.

"First, I was shocked to see how much tax I am paying – it's almost

35% of my income!" he exclaimed. "I guess I didn't realize how much it was since it is taken out of my paycheck every payday."

"Second, it was helpful for me to see where and how much I am spending every month. Since I have had plenty of money to live on and do the things I want to do, I haven't been too concerned with tracking my expenses. I guess the other insight is that I'm amazed at how my expenses have gone up as my income has gone up over the years," he added.

Will told him his insights were correct.

"Taxes are typically the biggest expense for a doctor, especially one who receives their income as W-2 wages," he said, adding that W-2 employees get very few deductions other than mortgage interest, state income and property taxes, and charitable contributions.

"And yes, you are correct in that you haven't needed to track your expenses in the past, but if you want to own your own medical clinic or clinics someday, you are going to need to start tracking expenses more regularly in order to make sure your business is profitable," Will noted.

"We call that a Profit & Loss Statement in the case of a business," he continued. "Regarding your insight about your expenses increasing, it is very common in the case of professionals if they are not intentional and disciplined about controlling expenses."

He called it "The Rat Race."

"Typically, the Rat Race happens when the more income you have, the more things there are to spend the income on," he explained. "You try and keep up with your peers and colleagues by spending like you assume they spend. Expenses start creeping up and up without being aware of it, and before you know it, you have developed bad spending habits."

He told Benjamin it was like the story of a frog in warm versus hot water.

"If you put a frog in hot water, it will jump out immediately, but if you put the frog in warm water and heat the water slowly, you can boil the frog – it does not perceive the danger and it will fully cook itself," Will said.

"That is how a lot of doctors develop bad financial or spending habits over time. If you want to achieve financial independence as quickly as possible and escape the Rat Race, it is important to identify and eliminate any poor financial habits as soon as you can and replace them with good habits."

It made a lot of sense to Benjamin. "But how do I do that?" he asked.

Will told him he'd have to create and maintain an Allocated Spending Plan. It would allow him to better control how he spends his money, he said.

"The purpose of this exercise is to start identifying any bad habits that need to be eliminated and start learning good habits that will help you more likely reach your financial goals," he explained.

He told him one of the first habits to develop is to start saying "No" to certain expenses and establishing a disciplined approach to saving and spending.

"As the saying goes, you want to learn to 'throw nickels around like they're manhole covers,'" he said, explaining that he needed to learn how to be stingy, like he was a resident and had limited income to spend on things.

"That sounds easier said than done," exclaimed Benjamin.

"It definitely requires work and building up your financial intelligence," Will responded, "which is why we build it into The Strategic Wealth System™ to help our clients increase the chances of financial success."

He said some clients also needed to reduce their high-interest debt, and that they had a Debt Reduction Plan that prioritizes which loans need to be repaid.

Will paused and asked Benjamin if he realized the importance of a Cash Flow Statement, an Allocated Spending Plan, and a Debt Reduction Plan.

"I do now," Benjamin replied, "especially in the case of getting ready to own and operate a business."

"Good," Will noted.

He announced that they'd focus on the second part of the discussion which was on controlling cash flow – focusing on assets and liabilities. He said they'd show it through a personal Net Worth Statement.

He started by telling Benjamin that his journey to financial intelligence requires that he knows how to calculate his true net worth.

He told Benjamin there's a conventional method to do this, which is mostly used by banks, and another way that the wealthy use.

"*The Richest Doctor* focuses on assets that only generate passive or portfolio income – their true net worth only includes assets that generate passive or portfolio types of income – called 'Investible Net Worth'," he explained.

He suggested examining the traditional method of calculating net worth in order to understand the difference between Conventional Net Worth and Investible Net Worth. He said it'd help him understand the numbers.

"Let's look at your list of everything you consider an asset and what it is approximately worth," he said, pulling up Benjamin's assets on the screen.

Benjamin's Assets	
Checking Account	$15,000
Savings Account	$17,750
Stocks and Bonds	$23,500
IRA	$38,000
401(k)	$74,750
Condo	$460,000
Automobile	$55,000
Home Furnishings	$65,000
Personal Belongings	$40,000

"All of my assets total up to $789,000," Benjamin announced.

Will said it was impressive. "Now let's look at your list of liabilities."

He pulled up Benjamin's liabilities then paused to digest the information.

Benjamin's Liabilities	
Mortgage on Condo	$430,000
Automobile Loan	$50,000
Credit Cards	$4,000

After a while, he moved on with the presentation. "Let's net these numbers together to come up with your net worth using the traditional method," he said.

Benjamin's Conventional Net Worth	
Total Assets	$789,000
- Total Liabilities	($484,000)
= Net Worth	$305,000

Benjamin's Investible Net Worth	
Checking Account	$15,000
Savings Account	$17,750
Stocks and Bonds	$23,500
IRA	$38,000
401(k)	$74,750
Investible Net Worth	$169,000

After taking a look at Benjamin's Investible Net Worth, Will said they had some recommendations for him based on his Net Worth Statement.

Cash Flow Recommendations for Benjamin	
1	Make sure you pay off your credit card each month to avoid paying the high interest.
2	Build up your savings account to $100,000 so that you have about 6 months of living expenses in case of an emergency.

"Even though it is unlikely that you would be out of work for six months, there are other reasons to have a healthy amount of liquid savings," he said. "Perhaps the biggest reason is to have a reserve to fund the start-up of your new business."

He added that although Benjamin would be able to fund most of his business' start-up expenses with the Small Business Administration (SBA) loan, it would be prudent to have cash to fund expenses if they exceed the loan proceeds.

"If we've learned anything living through the pandemic, it is that we can't predict when catastrophic events will occur that could impact our livelihood," Will said. "One other reason to maintain a substantial amount of cash is to be in a better position to take advantage of buying opportunities that may arise. If you have enough money on hand, you can jump at investment opportunities more effectively than if you had to rely on debt or need to pass because you didn't have cash reserves."

It made a lot of sense to Benjamin.

Will continued, "One lesson I've learned over the years is that having money in the bank has me sleep much better at night," he said. "One of the most stressful times was when unexpected expenses would come up and I didn't have the money to pay them."

"That is wise advice – expect the unexpected," his guest added.

Then Will explained why the conventional method is not a good way to measure how well one is doing in reaching their dream of achieving financial independence.

"Let's look at your condo that is worth approximately $460,000 with an outstanding mortgage of $430,000. What would happen if you lost your job tomorrow and couldn't find a new one for quite a while? Do you think you would be able to take out a second mortgage on the equity?" he asked.

"Probably not because I no longer have an income to pay the first mortgage," Benjamin answered.

"Precisely," Will replied. "Your condo becomes a pretend asset. All of a sudden, this condo you thought was your main asset is now a big, fat liability and you're stuck with it."

"We see clients get into financial trouble over and over because they were told their home was their biggest asset, and they figured they should buy the biggest home they could buy," he told Benjamin. "Just look at what happened in the 2008 recession. So many people owned homes where their mortgage exceeded the value of the home."

"Wow, I never thought of it that way," Benjamin observed.

"That's why the old saying goes, 'If you're starving, you can't eat your house.'" Will responded.

He told Benjamin that the same saying applies to automobiles. He said like homes, they are liabilities.

"An asset, as far as how the wealthy define net worth, puts money in your pocket," he said. "You can take that money and buy groceries. That is an asset. If it can feed you, it's an asset."

He said liabilities starve you on the other hand.

"They take money out of your pocket. They can destroy you. Your condo is not your biggest asset – rather, it's a liability," he said. "If something goes wrong, suddenly you are working for the mortgage company."

He called it financial imprisonment.

"Now you're working to pay for something that somebody else owns. The asset is the actual mortgage, which is the bank's asset, not yours. And credit cards are the worst if you don't pay them off every month – when you make a payment, you pay the interest first instead of paying down the principal. That also results in financial imprisonment," he explained.

"Unless you could sell all of your non-investible assets, pay off all of your liabilities, and have enough left over to buy another home, furnishings, and a vehicle with cash, you should not use these assets in calculating your net worth," Will advised.

He told Benjamin that he uses a simple rule when it comes to liabilities.

"You want to make sure that you have enough income-producing assets to cover your liabilities. We'll talk more about what income-producing assets are in a moment," he said.

"Wait a minute," Benjamin said, "I was also told that owning a home was a good investment."

"It may or may not be," Will responded. "Home ownership is not a bad thing. What I'm saying is that you don't want to buy a liability with another liability."

"I'm going to show you how to own your home but not so that it is

64

somebody else's asset and you're just paying them," he added.

Then he suggested they look at things from a Cash Flow Statement and Net Worth Statement perspective.

"Financially successful people acquire income-producing assets," he pointed out, adding that other people acquire liabilities that they think are assets.

"The difference between an asset and a liability is based on whether the cash flow flows through income or expenses. If cash flow is reported as income, it is an asset. If it is reported as an expense, it is a liability."

He produced a chart to explain how cash flow works for an asset.

——— Cash Flow Statements vs. Net Worth Statements ———

Cash Flow Statement	Net Worth Statement	
Income *Examples include:* Rents Interest Royalties Dividends	**Assets** *Examples include:* Rent Properties Stocks Bonds Notes	**Liabilities** *Examples include:* Mortgage Consumer Loans Student Loans Credit Cards
Expenses *Examples include:* Taxes Transportation Rent Clothing Food		

"The left part of this is what a Cash Flow Statement may look like in practice, or what is called a Profit & Loss Statement for a business," he said, adding that a Cash Flow Statement measures income and expenses like money coming in and money going out.

"The right part is a Net Worth Statement, or what may also be called a Balance Sheet for a business. It shows your assets, liabilities, and net equity or net worth," he added, pulling up a diagram that shows cash flow for a liability.

He explained that the diagrams show that an asset is something that puts money in one's bank account whether they work or not. Meanwhile, a liability is something that takes money out of one's bank account.

"If you want to achieve financial independence as quickly as possible, simply focus on buying and building assets instead of buying liabilities," he said.

He pulled up a new set of diagrams to show the difference between the financial statements of *The Richest Doctor* from a struggling doctor.

———————— *The Richest Doctor's* Cash Flow Statements vs. ————————
Net Worth Statements

The Richest Doctor's
Cash Flow Statement

Income
Expenses

Ordinary Doctor's
Cash Flow Statement

Income
Expenses

The Richest Doctor's
Cash Flow Statement

Assets
Liabilities

Ordinary Doctor's
Cash Flow Statement

Liabilities
Assets

"Which of these diagrams would you prefer to have?" he asked Benjamin.

"*The Richest Doctor's*, of course!" the latter responded.

The CPA explained why he earlier said Benjamin's home may not be an asset.

"For most people, owning a home is their dream, as well as their initial biggest investment," he started. "The bigger the home, the bigger the expenses."

"The notion that a home is a liability rather than an asset is not one that is widely accepted because home ownership is a very emotional investment," he pointed out.

"It is also counter to what most people hear from realtors and lenders who say 'your home is an asset,' or 'your house is your biggest investment,' or 'you get a tax break for going into more debt.' To the extent that the cost of owning a home prevents a person from buying income-producing assets, the home becomes a liability."

He added that buying an expensive dream home in lieu of building an income-producing investment portfolio impacts one in several ways.

"Let's look at them," he said, bringing up a new slide.

- First, it results in a *loss of time* during which other assets could have grown in value.
- Second, it results in a *loss of additional capital* which could have been invested rather than used for paying the high cost of home ownership and maintenance.
- Third, it results in a *loss of financial education and experience*.

"Too often, doctors have deferred their gratification for so long that they feel the need to buy the biggest home they can afford to make up for the lost years of being a poor medical student," he pointed out.

"They mistakenly see their home as an investment. They have no extra money to invest since their home expenses are so high, so as a result, they simply don't invest. This costs them investment experience and keeps them from building financial intelligence," he said.

"So, should I not buy a house?" Benjamin queried.

"No," Will answered, "That's not what I'm saying. What I'm saying is that you should understand the difference between an asset and a liability."

"If you want a more expensive house, you should first, or at the same time, make sure you have enough cash flow to buy assets that will generate cash flow to pay for the house," he explained. "Doctors who buy more houses than they should typically don't have enough savings after all their expenses to invest in other assets."

"Anyone who purchases a less expensive house than what they can afford has a better chance of having additional savings to invest," he said. "Just because you qualify for a large mortgage doesn't mean you should get one."

Some good advice is that the goal should be to buy a house that is between two and three times one's income, one should put at least 20% down, and then keep one's total home expenses between 20% and 25% of your net, after-tax, income.

"Can we take a look at my housing costs?" Benjamin asked.

Benjamin's Housing Costs	
Mortgage Payment	$3,512
Condo Association Dues	$35
Utilities	$1,105
Total Housing Cost	$4,652
Gross Income	$33,562
Less Taxes	$11,721
Net Income	$21,841
% Net Income Spent on Housing	21%

"Sure. You're in the recommended range, which is good," Will observed.

"Whew," Benjamin exclaimed, "I thought maybe I had already made a bad mistake."

Will decided now was the perfect time to fully explain a truer indication of net worth, as opposed to the more common and conventional method.

"The conventional method of net worth includes the value of assets such as your house, furnishings, personal belongings, and your automobile," he said. "If we are trying to determine the amount of assets you need to be financially independent, these assets – your home, car, and other stuff – are probably not going to be available to generate income during retirement."

"So, we need to remove them from the equation unless, of course, you plan to downsize your home and sell your possessions when you retire, which most people don't or can't do," he explained. "When we calculate your true net worth for purposes of defining financial independence, we focus on the types of assets we discussed earlier that generate income or can be sold at a gain."

"Depending on how well your new clinic performs, and if you can sell it or turn it into a passive income investment, you can include the value of your clinic as an asset," he added.

Will said they'd like to identify liabilities that needed to be paid off when Benjamin reaches his retirement years.

"As a general rule, debt that is not associated with an income-producing asset should be paid off by retirement, whereas debt that is incurred to purchase an asset that generates an amount of income that exceeds the debt service may be kept," he explained.

It was clear to Benjamin. "In other words, if I have a mortgage on my house and an outstanding business loan on my clinic in which the net profits of the clinic cover the loan payments, it would make sense to at least pay off the mortgage first, correct?" he asked.

"Correct," Will replied.

Step 4: Seek Wise Counsel

To start this session, Will told Benjamin that the next important lesson to learn was seeking counsel in investment decisions.

"Our culture teaches us to be a rugged individualist who makes decisions alone and unafraid, coping with any financial pressure in stoic silence," he said. "We are taught to be our own person – stand on your own two feet; you don't need anyone to tell you what to do."

He added that this teaching is further extended with highly educated professionals who believe they are smarter or more educated than everyone else, especially in light of the younger generation of do-it-yourselfers.

"Seeking advice regarding tax, investment, and business matters could save untold hours of self-learning and the cost of experiencing trials and errors," he pointed out.

> *"The way of a fool is right in his own eyes, But he who heeds counsel is wise."*
>
> *– Proverbs 12:15 NKJV*

"In my experience, the vast majority of doctors who have experienced financial difficulties or failed investments have not sought wise counsel beforehand," he said.

"They were molded by our culture's view that showing vulnerability and asking for advice is only for those who are not intelligent enough to be self-sufficient."

Benjamin spoke up. "I have heard about several horror stories of colleagues who thought they knew everything about an investment, only to find out they didn't when they lost money."

Will agreed with him, "Yes, that is a far too common reality."

"Moreover," he continued, "a doctor's pride is sometimes the biggest deterrent to seeking advice. It is embarrassing to expose our lack of knowledge to someone else."

"Another reason for the reluctance to seek advice is the fear that it may expose issues we would rather avoid – a lack of disciplined spending, an unrealistic budget, a lack of communication in the family, or a suggestion to give up something near and dear to us."

"Be careful from whom you take advice," he said. "It is best to find someone who has already taken the journey, especially in the areas of business and investing. A wise counselor is someone who tells you what is important and what is not important and helps you avoid making costly mistakes."

In all of the sessions he'd had with the Motley Crew, Will had asked the group to be cautious of the counsel of the biased. Whenever they were receiving financial or business advice, they should ask themselves one question:

"What stake does this person have in the outcome of my decision?"

He said if the advisor will profit or benefit from his or her advice, they should always seek an unbiased second or third opinion.

"You should try to obtain advice from many counselors. Proverbs 15:22 reads, 'Plans fail for lack of counsel, but with many advisers they succeed' (NIV). And Proverbs 11:14 (WEB) says, 'Where there is no wise guidance, the nation falls, but in multitude of counselors there is victory.'"

Will said the older he became, the more he recognized his need for many counselors.

"Each of us has a limited range of knowledge and experience, and we need others, with their own unique backgrounds, to give us insights and alternatives we never would have considered without their advice," he said.

He quoted King Solomon, in Ecclesiastes 4:9-12, which describes the benefits of dependence on one another in one of his favorite passages.

Two are better than one because they have a good return for their labor. If either of them falls down, one can help the other up. But pity anyone who falls and has no one to help them up...Though one may be overpowered, two can defend themselves. A cord of three strands is not quickly broken. (NIV)

"I suggest that you make a list of potential counselors you know who can provide you with objective advice, then rank each of them in the various areas of knowledge and experience," he told the group.

They could consider categories like general finances, savings and investments, business, and real estate.

"Estimate their level of experience from 1 to 5, 5 being most, in each of these areas," he said. "If you do not have someone who is either a 4 or 5 in any category, I suggest you ask your friends and family if they know someone whom you could talk to."

He also recommended that they should have at least two or three in each category so that they could benefit from several perspectives each advisor could provide.

Step 5: Understand Risk, and

Step 6: Build Tax-Efficient Wealth

Will turned to Benjamin. He clicked his mouse, "While we are talking about counsel and advice, let's talk about investments. That's where most people want and seek advice. Understanding investment risk depends on a number of factors, including these."

- What type of investor you are
- What do you plan to invest in
- How much time you are willing to spend to learn

What Type of Investor Are You?

He said when it came to understanding investment risk, one of the first questions to ask is "What type of investor are you or do you want to be?"

He explained that the type of investor one is dictates the type of risk one must deal with and how to manage the risk.

At Provident, we categorize investors into five general types.

Level 1: 'Too Busy to Learn' Level

The first investor type is the one who is too busy to learn about investing, Will stated.

"Many doctors at this level are highly intelligent people who are too busy with their careers, family, other interests, hobbies, and/or vacations," he said. "They would prefer to turn their money over to a financial advisor or institution to manage it for them."

He said they typically employ a professional investment advisor to diversify their investment portfolio or invest in a fund with a financial institution in exchange for a fee.

He went on, "We like the Rule of 100 as it relates to asset allocation. The Rule of 100 is a guideline of an investment portfolio to determine what percentage should be invested in a stock portfolio and a bond portfolio. If you subtract your age from 100, this is the percentage of your investment portfolio that should be allocated to a diversified stock portfolio."

Will said the remaining percentage should be allocated to a diversified U.S. bond portfolio.

"We suggest spreading the stock portfolio over three to seven asset classes with no more than 40% nor less than 5% in any one asset class, and in which between 20% and 50% is in international stock," he said.

"If you choose to work with a professional advisor, they can help you choose the proper asset allocation among specific stock and bond investments based on your goals, risk tolerance, and time horizon, then regularly rebalance the portfolio over your investment time horizon," Will added.

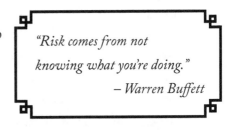

"Risk comes from not knowing what you're doing."
– Warren Buffett

He said if an institutional fund manager is chosen, it is important to select funds which are allocated over appropriate asset classes to maximize one's overall return with minimal portfolio risk.

"We also caution our clients from trying to time the stock market if they fall into this level. It is extraordinarily difficult to beat the market unless you are willing to spend a significant amount of time learning about short-term trading," he noted.

He said Benjamin should know that more than 90 percent of investment trading is done by professional investors who have far more talent, knowledge, and access to information than a typical doctor has.

"Unfortunately, this category of investor also attracts a lot of people who invest in speculative investments with very little time spent learning or researching about the investment," he said. "This type of investing is basically a form of gambling, typically in investments such as cryptocurrency, options, and leveraged ETF funds, and in most cases, results in disappointing losses."

He said it's not perfect timing in the market that works for most people but overall time in the market.

"If you research the stock market crash of 2000, you will see that it took 13 years before the markets came back to the level that they were at in 2000. In fact, the S&P 500 is one of the best long-term investments out there, and famed Warren Buffet has long touted the S&P

500 as an ideal option," Will added.

He said during the 2020 Berkshire Hathaway shareholder's meeting, Buffett claimed that "for most people, the best thing to do is to own the S&P 500 index fund."

Then he listed some of his favorite reasons why he thinks the S&P 500 generates good returns.

- The S&P 500 contains some of the strongest companies in the country, so it's more likely to see positive long-term growth.

- It is more resilient in the face of market crashes.

- Since the S&P 500's inception in 1957, it has earned an average rate of return of around 10% per year.

Will brought up a graph to corroborate the last reason.

———— S&P 500 Performance Since 2008 *(from YCharts)* ————

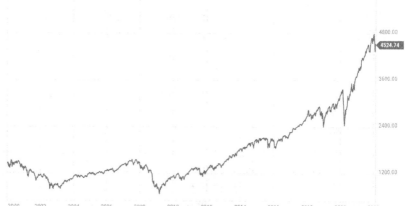

He took a chug of coffee and continued.

"Over the past 20 years, the S&P has grown by 194%, and the last decade, in particular, was an excellent decade to invest in the S&P 500. Since bottoming out in March 2009, the S&P 500 surged more than 370% through the end of 2019."

"For doctors who are not comfortable investing on their own, we recommend doctors in Level 1 to work with one or more independent fee-based financial advisors to develop your long-term investment strategy, and that the advisor helps you implement and periodically review the performance of your portfolio."

He said the more money one invests, the more often one should meet with them.

"Having a disciplined plan that you can stick with will keep you on track with focusing on your goals and minimize the risk of chasing overly risky or speculative investments," he said.

Level 2: Accredited Investor Level

Will proceeded to explain the next type of investor – the accredited investor. He said most doctors qualify as this type of investor early in their professional careers.

"If you meet certain requirements, you are permitted to make investments in securities that are not registered with the Securities and Exchange Commission (SEC)," he said. He added that all securities registered with the SEC are required to make certain disclosures to the SEC before they could be sold to the public.

"Unregistered securities are considered inherently riskier because they lack the normal disclosures that come with SEC registration," he explained.

According to him, an accredited investor in the United States must meet either the income test or the net worth test.

The income test requires an individual to have an annual income exceeding $200,000, or $300,000 for joint income with a spouse. It must be for the last two years, and they should be expecting to earn the same or higher income in the current year.

He explained that an individual must have earned income above the thresholds either alone or with a spouse over the last two years.

"The income test cannot be satisfied by showing one year of an individual's income and the next two years of joint income with a spouse," he explained. "The net worth test requires an individual to have a net worth exceeding $1 million, either individually or jointly with their spouse."

Will added that the purpose of the accredited investor requirements was to protect less knowledgeable individual investors who may not have the financial cushion to absorb losses or understand the risks associated with investments that are not registered with the SEC.

"Sellers of unregistered securities are only allowed to sell to accredited investors, who are deemed financially sophisticated enough to bear the risks," he added. "Clearly, merely having enough income or net worth to satisfy the requirement does not necessarily make someone financially sophisticated or know enough about investing enough to understand the risk associated with an unregistered investment."

Will explained that being an accredited investor may provide a false sense of security to a young doctor, especially one who has not yet developed financial intelligence about the underlying risks of such investments. He said they'd need to understand financial statements and projections and also conduct due diligence about the investment before making the investment.

"We highly recommend seeking advice from independent and objective experts who can educate you of the potential risks associated with the investment," he said.

According to Will, opportunistic investors sometimes get an early pick of the best investments where they can buy at very low prices, and in volume. He said it was one of the reasons why the wealthy became even wealthier.

"However, caution should always be exercised if you are an accredited investor to make sure you have the right knowledge and access to information before making the investment," he said.

"Our advice to a doctor is certainly not to put all of your eggs in one basket. Just like Level 1 investors, even if you qualify as an accredited investor, look at unregistered investments like a separate asset class and only put a portion of your overall investible net worth in non-publicly traded investments."

Level 3: Business Owner Level

The next level of investor is the Business Owner Level.

Will told Benjamin that it requires an entirely different kind of financial intelligence and education.

"Just like the education you received to become a doctor, you must be willing to obtain the business education necessary if you want to become a successful business owner," he said.

"The kind of education you need depends on the type of business," he added.

"In some cases, it may require you attend seminars and courses that can improve your business and investing skills. In other cases, personal development courses are available to develop real-life skills and give you the knowledge and operational skills to be a business owner," Will said.

According to him, owning a business sometimes requires raising capital from other investors. And knowing how to do this properly requires education on how to raise capital for a business opportunity.

He added that becoming a business owner requires a team of advisors. It is very important.

"No matter how smart you think you might be, having a team of experts and mentors is critical to avoiding the mistakes and problems that most businesses encounter. In most situations, two or three minds are better than one," he said.

He promised to discuss seeking counsel from experts and mentors with Benjamin at a later lesson (see 'Seek Wise Counsel').

Level 4: Real Estate Investor Level

Will started talking about the next investor level.

"Investing in rental real estate has become the latest fad for investors over the past decade," he said. "When I talk with many of our doctor clients, most of them believe rental real estate investing as the holy grail to building a passive income."

He said it is a dangerous assessment.

"The truth is most properties do not make good rental property investments. In our experience, more than 8 or 10 potential real estate investments do not pan out financially – the number is higher in hot real estate markets."

"Why is that?" asked Benjamin.

"Because the numbers don't work," Will responded. "What most people do not realize is that investing in real estate is a business – it is not passive income until you own enough real estate to hire people to run your real estate business."

He continued, "What did I mean when I said 'the numbers don't work'? It means that your actual expenses, which are typically more than what people realize, exceed the income on the property, and therefore, you lose money."

"The goal of investing is to make money, not lose it," he said. All risks involved with rental property are directly related to the numbers.

"Until you really understand the numbers and what actually goes into receiving positive cash flow, the risks will make all the more sense," he said, listing several ways to invest in real estate.

He said it could be through syndicated partnerships, real estate investment trusts, Delaware Statutory Trusts, or direct ownership.

He said he'd only talk about direct or outright ownership in rental real estate that one plans to hold onto for a long period of time with Benjamin.

Then he listed the most likely ways to lose money with real estate and rental properties.

Unpredictable Market

"The market plays a significant role in the future value of real estate properties," Will stated.

"Most people who make significant profits in real estate do so by buying at the right time. If you buy real estate during peak times, then you are going to have to own it for a potentially longer time to make a profit than if you buy it when prices are low," he said.

"The best way to avoid negative equity, in the case of a debt financing, was to thoroughly research and understand the market to avoid buying at peak prices," he said.

Poor Location

"There's a saying in real estate that goes, 'location, location, location'," Will started, adding that real estate investing wouldn't fit Benjamin if he hadn't heard that quip before.

"Choosing a good location is one of the first things investors should consider. While investing in a poor location may seem like a big risk, it can still make sense if the purchase price is low or if the neighborhood shows signs of future development," he said.

Negative Cash Flow

"The amount of profit left after making mortgage payments, expenses, and taxes on a real estate property is one's cash flow," Will said to Benjamin.

"If your rental income is less than your expenses, you have a problem – negative cash flow," he said. "Clearly you want positive cash flow when it comes to investment real estate since the whole reason you invested in the first place was to make a profit."

He told Benjamin that the best way to avoid negative cash flow is to decrease the amount of debt on the property by increasing the down payment and thoroughly calculating all expected and unexpected expenses before purchasing the property.

Decreasing Property Value or Rents

"If the neighborhood in which you purchase rental property experiences foreclosures and short sales, then the risk of the entire neighborhood losing value is high," Will said.

Will let him know that it is important to keep this in mind if he plans to buy, sell, or refinance any of his properties in these depressed neighborhoods.

"You don't want to be in a situation where the market for your property declines in such a way you are no longer able to cover your expenses with decreasing rental income," he said. "A few simple ways to avoid this risk is to only buy in a growth area in which values should go up and do not buy at the top of the market."

Unexpected Repairs and Maintenance

"The cost of fixing things with rental real estate can range all across the board and can sometimes cost more than the appreciation of the property value," Will explained to Benjamin.

"Some of the more serious expenses include roofs, structural issues, internal wiring, and problems you didn't know existed when you bought the property," he said.

He then listed several ways to minimize the risk of high costs of repairs and maintenance before buying the property. They were:

- Getting a detailed professional property inspection.
- Building the costs into the cash flow projections to make sure you can still have positive cash flow with the costs included.
- Investigate a prospective tenant's rental history and obtain a credit report to make sure they are high-quality renters.

Vacancy

"Vacancy poses a bigger issue than most buyers realize," Will said to Benjamin.

He advised him to always keep in mind that tenants can unexpectedly break a rental agreement at any time.

"Just look at what happened during the COVID-19 pandemic – there were a significant number of occurrences in which tenants broke their rental agreements due to their loss of employment, need to move, or for other reasons."

He told him to prepare for a few things during vacancies. They were:

- Lost rental income, which is critical if one has a mortgage on the property.
- Repairs incurred after the previous tenant.
- Payments to any leasing agent for the new tenant, which are usually approximately one month's rent.

Next, he listed a few ways to reduce the risk of unanticipated vacancies before buying a property:

- Buy in a growing market and where there are not a significant number of vacant properties.
- Research vacancy rates in the local market so you have an idea of what to expect.
- Don't purchase rental properties in a neighborhood in which only homeowners live.

- Maintain an ample cash surplus, such as six months of rental income, to help weather through extended periods of vacancy.

After running through the real estate investment materials, Will stopped the presentation and looked at Benjamin.

"Although this list of potential risks may seem daunting to a potential real estate investor, being aware of them should help mitigate the risk with caution and prudent steps taken," he said.

Then he proceeded to the level of investing that excited him the most.

Level 5: Serial Entrepreneur Level

"The top of the investor food chain is the serial entrepreneur level," Will stated.

He said they are the "tip of the spear" when it comes to their willingness to study and analyze business opportunities.

"This is an individual who owns several businesses and/or real estate investments," he elaborated further. "Many of them also have a portion of their net worth in traditional investments, such as tax-deferred retirement plans and after-tax investment portfolios and liquid savings. They consider their business and real estate portfolios as another asset class."

"Serial entrepreneurs are usually the kind of people who win at the game of Monopoly," he said, asking Benjamin if he knew how to win at Monopoly.

"No," Benjamin responded sheepishly, "I was never able to win when I played."

Will told him the secret of playing Monopoly. It is to buy green houses as quickly as possible. Then when one has four green houses, they should trade them for a large red hotel and then repeat the process over and over.

"Eventually, you own several hotels and collect maximum rent every time a player lands on your property with a hotel," he said, "The keys to becoming a serial entrepreneur are being intentional and having a plan, then taking one step at a time acquiring property or starting or buying a business that you can grow and sell someday."

He quoted Michael Gerber, author of *The E-Myth Revisited*: "The ultimate reason to create a business of your own is to sell it."

Then he listed more tips he believed Benjamin ought to know.

Characteristics of an Entrepreneur:

- The entrepreneur lives in the future, never in the past, rarely in the present. He is happiest when left free to construct images of "what-if" and "if-when."

- The entrepreneur is an innovator, the grand strategist, the creator of new methods for penetrating or creating new markets.

- The entrepreneur is our creative personality – always at its best dealing with the unknown, prodding the future, creating probabilities out of possibilities, engineering chaos into harmony.

- The entrepreneur has an extraordinary need for control. He needs control of people and events in the present so that he can concentrate on his dreams.

- The entrepreneur creates a great deal of havoc around him, which is predictably unsettling for those he enlists in his projects.

- The entrepreneur's worldview is a world made up of both an overabundance of opportunities and dragging feet.

- To the entrepreneur, most people are problems that get in the way of the dream.

"In summary, Gerber believes successful entrepreneurs are those who know how they got where they are and what they need to do to get where they're going; they have a vision for their lives that they practice emulating every day," he concluded.

"The difference between a successful entrepreneur and everyone else is that an entrepreneur creates their lives actively while everyone else is created by their lives, passively waiting to see where life takes them next."

What Do You Want to Invest In?

Will told Benjamin the next thing to ask is: "What should he invest in?"

He said the answer to this question depended on several factors, including what type of investor he is.

"If you are a Level 1 Investor (Too Busy to Learn), then your best course of action is to engage an independent investment advisor who can help you design an investment portfolio to meet your goals," he said.

"If you go the do-it-yourself route, then you should consider investing in an S&P index and/or target fund with an online financial advisory firm," he added.

He went on.

"If you fit the requirements for a Level 2 Investor (An Accredited Investor), then you may be a candidate to invest a portion – somewhere between 10% and 20% of your investible net worth among these options."

- Private placements
- Real estate syndications and limited partnerships
- Pre-initial public offerings (IPOs)
- Sub-prime financing
- Loans for start-up businesses
- Hedge funds

Will said these investments are too risky for an average investor, or one who is not willing to understand the risks or become financially intelligent. He said it wasn't because the investment itself was necessarily risky but because the average or unsophisticated investor lacked sufficient education and experience to understand how the investment operates.

"Investing in a business, which means you want to be a Level 3 (Business Owner) requires a different level of learning," he said.

"Our general rule of thumb for doctors interested in investing in a business is to only invest in what you know – the more you know about a business, the more likely that you can control the risk associated with the business."

How Much Time Are You Willing to Spend Learning?

To answer this question, Will spoke about something Robert Kiyosaki said in his book *Rich Dad's Guide to Investing*. He said people think investing is risky because of three primary reasons:

- They have not been trained to be investors.
- Most investors lack control or are out of control.
- Most people invest from the outside rather than from the inside.

Will started to explain what being trained to be an investor means.

"It means that you must spend a significant amount of time to become financially intelligent," he said.

"Financial intelligence means that you study what you are considering investing in inside and out. If it's a business, you study everything you can get your hands on to know the challenges and opportunities of the business and its industry, and you can read and understand financial statements."

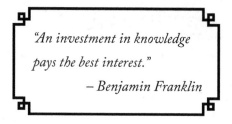

"An investment in knowledge pays the best interest."
– Benjamin Franklin

"Being in control of your investing means that you have a detailed plan, and you remain highly disciplined in following the plan and monitoring it regularly," he added.

Chapter 4

Five Years Later

The day finally arrived when the four friends from medical school were going to meet and share how the past five years had gone for each of them, discuss their successes and failures, and the lessons learned from them. They had agreed to meet at Will's office mid-morning, meet through a working lunch to late afternoon, then celebrate together over a nice dinner and drinks. Spouses were invited to join.

Benjamin was the first to arrive. He was so excited to introduce his new bride, Emily, to his friends. The newlyweds were a month away from their first anniversary, and they had recently received the great news that they were expecting their first child due in six months.

Joy and Elijah arrived shortly thereafter, followed by Serena and Josh, then Indira and Chatura. After 20 minutes of hugging, laughing, and small talk, Will and Mal entered the conference room.

"Welcome everyone," Will said with a raised voice over the rumble of conversations, "Please, everyone, help yourselves to coffee and refreshments in the back of the room and find your nametag around the conference room table and take a seat. We have prepared a personalized notebook for each of you that we'll review today."

Will continued, "As you all know, Mal and the rest of our team at Provident CPAs have been working with each of you over the past five years. We've been honored to work with you and appreciate all the hard work, discipline, and willingness to learn on the journey to financial independence. Each of you developed unique goals when we started five years ago. There were times when a couple of you didn't know if you could stay on track with your goals when unexpected events occurred, but I am proud to share that, though your paths differed, you have all been successful in your own way."

"It's not standard practice here, but each of you has agreed to share your progress with the others today, discuss what new goals you would like to set for the next five years, and discuss strategies on how to achieve them. Mal has compiled the results for each of you and prepared a report in each of your notebooks. Mal, would you please share with the group everyone's results and reports."

Mal responded, "Absolutely! Would everyone kindly open their notebook to the Table of Contents? As you can see, I have organized the notebook with a tab for each of you. What I would like to do is start with Elijah, then discuss Serena's, then Benjamin's, and finally, Indira's. At the end of each section, we will pause and let each of you share your insights, lessons learned, and struggles or obstacles faced over the past five years and how you overcame them, and any current issues that you would like to discuss as a group. We will plan to take a short break each hour and bring in lunch as we work. Does anyone have any questions?"

The members of the group shook their heads.

"Well, let's get started with Elijah," Mal continued.

Elijah's Progress

Elijah cleared his throat with a cough, then said, "The past five years have been an interesting time for Joy and me. I never realized how difficult it would be to come up with a financial game plan and stick with it. It seemed like it took about six months to come up with a budget that Joy and I could stick with. Our living expenses, especially raising four children, was the most challenging thing to nail down – every time we turned around, there was another unexpected expense or something we needed."

Elijah continued, "With Will's help and patience, we finally got a handle on our expenses and cash flow. I think the biggest insight was being disciplined to take out an amount from every paycheck that we planned to save, then separate out the things that we needed to buy versus the things that we didn't need but wanted. Those items that we wanted, we then ranked from top to bottom in order of importance.

Once we built up an emergency fund equal to six months of living expenses, only then would we see if we had additional cash flow after the amount we carved out for savings, giving, and our needs. If we had additional, we would buy those things we wanted. I also worked one to two extra moonlighting shifts each month and committed to put that money into an additional savings account which we invested with the assistance of Matt, the financial advisor Will introduced us to."

"As all of you know, my parents have worked as career employees for a university and state government agency, so I didn't have the upbringing around owning a business or investment properties. I didn't understand how to evaluate the risks of business and real estate ownership, so my investment portfolio stayed within a narrower range of safer investments. My financial advisor helped me establish a diversified portfolio of stocks and bonds which we rebalanced when necessary."

"To give you some background information," Elijah continued, "my base salary at the hospital started out at $400,000 five years ago, and I've received a 4% cost of living annual increase. Between my 403(b) and 457 plan, I contributed or had contributed on my behalf the maximum amount, which started at $58,000 per year. In addition, Joy and I contributed to our backdoor Roth IRAs each year. We were able to keep our lifestyle expenses at approximately $200,000, so we were able to invest our additional savings in a taxable investment account. After taking inflation into account, we have made an average annual return on all of our investments of 4%, which puts our current Investible Net Worth – which, by the way, was zero 5 years ago – at $595,636, shown on a chart in my section of the notebook."

Elijah's Investible Net Worth After 5 Years	
Tax-Free Retirement Accounts	$82,780
Tax-Deferred Retirement Accounts	$400,101
Taxable Investment Accounts	$267,338
Total Investments	$750,218
Less Deferred Income Taxes at 37%	($154,582)
Net Investible Net Worth	**$595,636**

"Congratulations!" shouted Indira as she clapped.

"Yes, that's really good!" confirmed Benjamin.

Will smiled and said to Elijah and Joy, "I know it was a bumpy road at first, but I take my hat off to both of you for coming together and doing the hard work necessary to get and keep your finances on track!"

"Thank you," declared Joy as Elijah nodded and took a deep breath and exhaled.

Will turned to his right. "Serena, would you like to be next to share your progress with the group, and then, Benjamin, do you want to be on deck?"

"Sure," replied Serena, "I'd be happy to."

Serena's Progress

Serena began, "Like Joy and Elijah, Josh and I struggled to get our finances in order at the beginning, especially with Josh's difficulty in getting back to work at a stable job. He ended up getting his master's degree and now has a management position at our local Amazon distribution center. With our three kids getting ready to start college, we are now able to start saving a portion of Josh's salary for their upcoming college expenses."

"Similar to Elijah, I have been blessed with a steady job at the hospital I work at, and I've been able to pick up several additional shifts every month moonlighting. I believe the biggest difference from Elijah is that I was able to change my employment relationship to an independent contractor relationship with the hospital I work for, as well as with the various side moonlighting gigs. Thanks to the tax planning that Will provided us, which was much like the recommendations that he created for Benjamin and Indira, we have been able to significantly reduce the amount of income and payroll taxes we owe, which we have in turn been able to save."

Benjamin and Indira looked at each other and grinned as they nodded their heads in agreement. Together with Serena, they all knew the benefit of having worked as 1099 contractors.

"My base income was the same as Elijah's over the past five years. Will helped me set up a couple of retirement plans for my PLLC that allowed me to contribute $100,000 each year, half of which went into

88

a tax-deferred account and the other half into a tax-free account. In addition, we contributed to our backdoor Roth IRA each year. By keeping our lifestyle spending low, and thanks to the tax savings Will provided, we had more money to save on other investments. Elijah and I both hired the same financial advisor, Matt, to manage our investments. My after-inflation return was similar to Elijah's, which resulted in the following Investible Net Worth."

Serena's Investible Net Worth After 5 Years	
Tax-Free Retirement Accounts	$427,694
Tax-Deferred Retirement Accounts	$344,915
Taxable Investment Accounts	$263,613
Total Investments	$1,036,222
Less Deferred Income Taxes at 37%	($134,072)
Net Investible Net Worth	**$902,150**

"Bravo!" chimed Benjamin.

"That's amazing!" Indira sang out as the group juxtaposed Elijah's and Serena's financial progress.

"Let's compare Elijah's and Serena's Investible Net Worth charts," interjected Will. "We'll be making these comparisons throughout the presentations because I want to show you what certain changes that are implemented can do to change the long-term outcome. Each of you is approaching your financial independence differently but have time to make adjustments if you see that one of your colleague's paths is more desirable than your own."

Comparing Elijah's and Serena's Investible Net Worth After 5 Years	
Serena	$902,150
Elijah	$595,636
Difference in dollars	$306,513
Difference in percentage	151%

Comparing Elijah's and Serena's After-Tax Retirement Income Using the 4% Rule at Year 5	
Serena	$36,086
Elijah	$23,825
Difference in dollars	$12,261
Difference in percentage	151%

Why Did Serena Have Better Results Than Elijah?

Elijah asked, "Why exactly did Serena have better results than me in the amount of Investible Net Worth and also retirement income?"

"Good question, Elijah. Let's look at some of the differences between what you and Serena did over the past five years," replied Will. "The biggest difference between your plan and Serena's is that she was able to save a significant amount of taxes because of her PLLC and being able to take advantage of all of the available business tax deductions. That additional tax savings was able to then be invested. Our tax system favors businesses much more than individuals. W-2 employees are especially disadvantaged – they pay more in payroll taxes and don't get the tax deductions available to business owners."

Elijah replied morosely, "That's frustrating. It seems unfair for those of us who are employees to have to pay more than those who are able to be independent contractors."

"I agree," said Will, "that is why we encourage our clients to own a business if they can – even if it merely involves changing your employment status to being an independent contractor. In your case, you attempted to do that with the hospital five years ago, but they refused. In our experience, the bigger and more bureaucratic a hospital, the less flexible and willing they are to help their doctor-employees. They somehow think that they lose control if they allow a doctor to be an independent contractor rather than an employee."

Elijah responded with evident annoyance, "It's hard enough that we have to put up with so many regulations and red tape in our industry, that we have to pay so much in taxes."

Everyone in the group nodded in empathy.

"Perhaps we can explore if you can arrange your moonlighting gigs as an independent contractor status," Will said. "If so, you'll be able to realize many of the same tax benefits by being able to set up the right tax structure. Let's take a 10-minute break, then come back and hear from Benjamin."

Benjamin's Progress

Benjamin was scribbling notes in his notebook as the group gathered back in the conference room.

"If everyone is ready, let's begin," announced Will.

"Benjamin, are you ready to share how the past five years have been and any insights you learned?"

"Sure," Benjamin replied. "When I wrote down my goals five years ago, I wrote that I wanted to start or invest in a side business to supplement my salary at the hospital. I had the benefit of having two groups of entrepreneurs in my family – my parents who owned a successful dry-cleaning business and my aunt and uncle who owned a multi-office chiropractic practice. With the help of them and Will, I researched several different business ventures and ended up with one in my own industry that looked promising – an urgent care clinic in my community. After conducting a thorough demographic and psychographic study, I put together a business plan with financial projections and applied for and received a $1 million SBA loan to fund the start-up costs. As a side note, I followed Serena's path and converted my W-2 employee status into an independent contractor and established a PLLC so that I could take advantage of the tax planning strategies recommended by Will."

"I started the clinic a year later, and this year, we broke even from a cumulative net cash flow standpoint. Revenues this year reached $1 million and net profits were 20%. I hired an associate physician to work in the clinic and offered him the opportunity to purchase a 49% interest in the clinic next year that will be valued at five times net earnings and paid in the form of a promissory note over 10 years. I also plan to have a buy-sell agreement to allow her to buy my remaining 51% interest in the event something happens to me. I plan to open my second clinic next year in a nearby community and structure it the same way as the first clinic. I also funded my business and individual retirement accounts like Serena, and with Will's assistance, saved my surplus net cash flow in a taxable investment account. I also hired Matt, the same financial advisor who helped Elijah and Serena, to help me manage my investments. You can see how my Investible Net Worth is doing in the chart."

Benjamin's Investible Net Worth After 5 Years	
Tax-Free Retirement Accounts	$427,694
Tax-Deferred Retirement Accounts	$344,915
Taxable Investment Accounts	$593,232
Business Interests	$59,036
Total Investments	$1,424,877
Less Deferred Income Taxes at 37%	($134,072)
Net Investible Net Worth	**$1,290,805**

"That's fantastic!" Serena proclaimed. "I am so impressed with your entrepreneurial spirit and willingness to jump into owning your own business."

"Thanks, I appreciate that!" replied Benjamin with a sheepish grin.

Will said, "Now, let's compare how Benjamin did compared to Serena over the past two years."

Comparing Serena's and Benjamin's Investible Net Worth After 5 Years	
Benjamin	$1,290,805
Serena	$902,150
Difference in dollars	$388,655
Difference in percentage	143%

Comparing Serena's and Benjamin's After-Tax Retirement Income Using the 4% Rule at Year 5	
Benjamin	$132,976
Serena	$36,086
Difference in dollars	$96,890
Difference in percentage	368%

Why Did Benjamin Have Better Results Than Serena?

"Why did Benjamin have better results than Serena?" asked Elijah with a puzzled look on his face.

Indira jumped in, "Is it because Benjamin invested in a business that he would sell someday whereas Serena just had 1099 income?"

Will replied, "That's correct! Benjamin, tell the group what your biggest insights and lessons learned in your journey to achieve financial independence so far."

Benjamin answered, "Thanks to my entrepreneurial family and Will, who is one of the wisest entrepreneurs I have met, I've had some big insights and revelations over the past five years. I had Mal put them in the notebook on the last page of my section."

Ben's List

- I narrowed my choice of businesses and industry to something that I already knew about.

- I sought out objective and wise mentors and advisors who had experience in building successful businesses.

- I dedicated myself to learning everything I could about this business and what it takes to make it successful before I made the investment in the business.

- I prepared a detailed business and financial plan and ran multiple scenarios based on varying assumptions.

- I created the right business structure so I could make the most of tax write-offs that allowed me to shelter most, if not all, the net profits from the business from unnecessary income taxes.

- I adopted and applied the Entrepreneurial Operating System® in my first clinic, and it will be a part of my second clinic and all clinics going forward.

- I built a business that I could sell someday but have a plan to convert it into a passive income-generating investment.

- I kept my lifestyle expenses low so that I could reinvest excess cash flow into the business, pay off debt, and/or make other investments. Emily says that I now, as the saying goes, 'throw nickels around like they're manhole covers,' which isn't always her favorite thing, but she sees the value."

Emily nodded and grinned when she read the last bullet point.

"Well done!" cheered Indira after everyone finished reading. "I am very impressed with your dedication and commitment!"

Turning to Indira, Benjamin said, "Well, I couldn't have done it alone – I owe a lot to my mentors and advisors. They saved me thousands of dollars and kept me from making more mistakes. And I especially appreciate the time we spent together learning from each other!"

Indira smiled, "The feeling is mutual."

"Good presentation," proclaimed Will. "After a short break, we will next hear from Indira."

Indira's Progress

When the group returned to the conference room, everyone's preferred lunch and drink choices were waiting for them on the table.

"I am honored to be with all of you today," Indira quietly said looking at each person. "The past five years have passed so quickly for me. Shortly after our last meeting five years ago, Will helped me put my goals into action, then guided me all along the way. Fortunately, Benjamin and I had a similar goal of starting an urgent care clinic during the first year. Last year, I also started a second business – a locum tenens service that connects independent contractor physicians and physician assistants with local hospitals and clinics. Thanks to my parents, Benjamin's parents, and my aunt and uncle, I thoroughly researched and studied several business models on how to start and build a successful business."

"The primary difference between Benjamin and myself regarding our clinics is that I also purchased the land and building for the clinic. Similar to Benjamin, I am currently in the due diligence phase of looking for a location for a second clinic. I also converted my W-2 status with the hospital into an independent contractor through my PLLC, fully funded my business and individual retirement accounts, and had the surplus cash flow to fund other investments as a result of the tax planning strategies that Will provided. My Investible Net Worth is on the first page after the tab in the notebook."

Indira's Investible Net Worth After 5 Years	
Tax-Free Retirement Accounts	$427,694
Tax-Deferred Retirement Accounts	$344,915
Taxable Investment Accounts	$636,247
Business Interests	$59,036
Real Estate Interest	$978,207
Total Investments	$2,446,099
Less Deferred Income Taxes at 37%	($134,072)
Net Investible Net Worth	**$2,312,027**

Benjamin was the first to respond, "Wow, Congratulations, Indira! Looks like you took home the gold medal."

Indira, looking down somewhat embarrassed, "I certainly couldn't have done it myself. I had a lot of help along the way."

Will added, "With your permission, Benjamin, may we examine Indira's progress compared to yours?"

"Sure. I think there are probably some lessons for me to learn in this comparison."

Comparing Benjamin's and Indira's Investible Net Worth After 5 Years	
Indira	$2,312,027
Benjamin	$1,290,805
Difference in dollars	$1,021,223
Difference in percentage	179%

Comparing Benjamin's and Indira's After-Tax Retirement Income Using the 4% Rule at Year 5	
Indira	$151,965
Benjamin	$132,976
Difference in dollars	$8,988
Difference in percentage	114%

Why Did Indira Have Better Results Than Benjamin?

"How did you do so much better than Benjamin and the rest of us?" asked Elijah.

Indira replied, "It certainly wasn't easy. I made plenty of mistakes, but every time, when something went wrong, I tried to turn it into a learning experience. I set up regular meetings with Will and my mentors to seek their advice."

"The biggest difference between my results and Benjamin's results was that I acquired the real estate in which each of my clinics was located. Rather than paying rent to someone else, I paid rent to myself which allowed me to pay off the mortgage I took out on each property. I also attribute my business success to implementing the Entrepreneurial Operating System® or EOS. Everyone in my organization now drinks the EOS Kool-Aid!"

"That's the second time I've heard this thing called the Entrepreneurial Operating System™ – both you and Benjamin. What exactly is it?" asked Serena.

Indira responded, "I'll defer to Will to explain it over dinner tonight, which by the way, will be on me!"

Later that evening, Will explained, "Every business has an operating system, whether or not it is written and whether or not it is followed by everyone in the organization. According to Gino Wickman, author of the best-selling book *Traction*, if you're like most business owners, you have probably experienced, or will experience, one or more of some common frustrations."

"I just happened to bring a few copies of an EOS worksheet for you all," said Will.

- *Lack of control over your time, the market, or your business* – instead of controlling your business, your business controls you.

- *Frustration with your employees, customers, patients, vendors, or partners* – who don't seem to listen or understand you or follow through with their actions.

- *Not profitable enough.*

- *You hit the ceiling* – no matter what you do, you can't seem to break through and get to the next level.

- *Nothing seems to work* – you're spinning your wheels.

The EOS has six components that make up any business. It's important to understand and get these right to be successful.

The Vision Component – which focuses on getting everyone in an organization to see where the business is going and how it's going to get there and asks the following eight questions:

1. What are your core values?

2. What is your core focus?

3. What is your 10-year target?

4. What is your marketing strategy?

5. What is your 3-year picture?

6. What is your 1-year plan?

7. What are your quarterly Rocks (the most important things to get done over the next 90 days)?

8. What are your issues?

"In their book, *Built to Last*, Jim Collins and Jerry Porras found that organizations that have endured for decades share a common practice. They all set massive 10- to 25-year goals. They refer to these as BHAGs – Big, Hairy, Audacious Goals – and define them as having 'a long-term vision so daring in scope as to seem impossible.'"

- *The People Component* – which focuses on getting an account-ability chart and putting the right people in the right seats in the organization.

- *The Data Component* – which focuses on monitoring the most important data and numbers of the organization.

- *The Issues Component* – which focuses on identifying the most important issues facing an organization, then prioritizing and solving them in a lasting and meaningful way.

- *The Process Component* – which focuses on identifying, address-ing, and documenting each of the core processes of an organi-zation, then making sure they are understood and followed by everyone in the organization.

- *The Traction Component* – focuses on "Rocks" – which are the most important things that need to be done in the next 90 days – and keeps everyone in the organization accountable, aligned, and in communication.

Will continued, "We have been using EOS at Provident CPAs consistently since our inception, which has resulted in faster growth, increased profitability, and great people that everyone in the organi-zation enjoys working with. Our growth rate has averaged more than 40% per year. *Traction* includes an Organizational Checkup that tells you exactly where your business is. You can also find the questionnaire online at https://organizationalcheckup.com/. If you are in, or are plan-ning to enter, the 'B' quadrant soon, I encourage you to read *Traction* and complete the Organization Checkup."

"Creating an operating system takes an enormous amount of time, and trial and error, until you get one that works. Adopting the EOS expedites the learning curve by allowing a business owner to 'plug and play' a proven operating system used by other successful organizations. Some organizations adopt and implement EOS by themselves. Others hire consultants who are EOS-trained. At Provident CPAs, we have dedicated in-house team members who are EOS-trained, and this approach has helped us stay on track."

"Getting everyone in an organization on the same page ensures that issues get resolved more quickly. In *The Five Dysfunctions of a Team*, Patrick Lencioni observed, 'If you could get all the people in an organization rowing in the same direction, you could dominate any industry, in any market, against any competition, at any time.' It's worth mentioning again the importance of having good systems and processes in your business in order to build and maintain a well-oiled machine."

In his best-selling book, *The E-Myth Revisited*, Michael Gerber re-iterates the importance of systems in a business when he said, "Systems run the business and people run the systems. Systems permit ordinary people to achieve extraordinary results predictably."

"To the degree you clarify and perfect your systems, you will run your business as opposed to your business running you. Having good systems and processes will increase the value of your business, strengthen your control over it, and give you freedom. Once you recognize the purpose of your life is not to serve your business, but have your business' purpose to serve your life, you can then start working on your business, rather than in it, with an understanding of why it is absolutely critical for you to do so."

Step 7: Focus on Progress, Not Perfection

"While we are sitting here over dinner, talking about business success and your personal successes, I want to pump the brakes a little bit," stated Will.

"Because our clientele is exclusively high-performance individuals that have pushed themselves and taken on the responsibilities with high-income careers, it's not unusual that they are perfectionists – or at least striving toward perfection. I want you all to know a key lesson to all of this. Sometimes you need to focus on the progress and not how close or far you are from perfection."

Will took a sip of wine and continued, "We talked about 'baby steps' five years ago. There's a reason I laid that foundation. As you've looked at your peers' financial performance over the past five years, it's easy to feel like you are falling behind, not on par, or not winning the race. That's not true. The key to all of this is progress, enjoying the journey, and reaching a place where you leave a legacy."

Benjamin, Indira, Serena, and Elijah, and their spouses looked around each other and wondered what had gotten into their trusty accountant.

"Before we meet again in five years, you'll have children leaving for college, new opportunities present themselves, and old opportunities not turn out as you expect. All along this way, it is about the journey. I wanted to give you some tips I've learned over the years," said Will.

"As I started my career, I had instances where I let perfection get in the way of progress. First, I want you to know that outcomes don't have to be classified as success or failure. There can be a gray area. If you reach 90% of a goal that you set, that is an opportunity to make an adjustment and secure that last 10%. But I've seen many perfectionists call that 90% result a failure, throw their hands up, and stop. It's my hope that gray area results aren't an end but an indicator to make adjustments."

"Next, I've seen perfectionists and those in pursuit of perfection slow down, lose energy and become paralyzed by self-criticism. Keep the baby steps and you'll keep a sense of advancing and succeeding. The biggest killer might be that living in a place of pessimism from chasing perfection can rob you of new ideas that could yield the idea that helps you change course and get closer to your goals."

"This actually makes a lot of sense," said Elijah. "I've seen some of my peers struggle when something doesn't go as they planned in the emergency room or even when they feel disrespected by hospital administration. I've never thought how it could apply to my financial picture."

"I've seen it too," said Benjamin. "I know you well enough by now, Will, to know that you have some tips on what is best to do in these situations. What are they?"

"I think it's easiest to say it this way – 'Believe in the progress, not the perfection'," said Will. "I've struggled with this throughout my career. I carry a card in my wallet that I can pull out and remind myself of some key truths about pursuing progress over perfection."

Will dug out his wallet from his back pocket, filed through some cards, and pulled out a laminated piece of paper with his handwriting. On the card, it said:

- Progress means motivation
- Progress means success
- Progress means improvement
- Progress means movement
- Progress is thriving on change

"For me, the two points remind me that making progress in your journey means you have a track record of success that you can remember. That motivates me. If you think back to our quarterly cycle – either our Quarterly Pulse we use to engage you or the quarterly pulse you use from EOS – both are cycles where you take time and remember the successes and set the course for the future, both of which are motivating behaviors." Will reflected.

"Improvement is important. Striving for progress over perfection means being in a mindset to learn from challenges and mark more things up as learning experiences and not moments of failure. Also, progress is movement. As long as you are putting effort and intention into your journey, you will move forward. The pace may not be as quick as you would like, but progress is movement toward a better outcome."

"Finally, it's important to remember that progress is thriving on change," said Will. "With a progress over perfection mindset, you'll be more open to the changes that get thrown our way on a journey. I've found that being able to change course sometimes gives you something even better than what you imagined. Once, I was presented with an opportunity to merge with a colleague's firm. As we investigated the opportunity, I found that our values didn't align, and it wasn't a good fit. The other firm eventually dissolved. But that experience and journey helped us define what we were looking for in the core values and beliefs of our team members and future team members. In essence, we thrived by ending up in a better position and smarter. This plays out all the time in adjusting with financial opportunities, investments, and more."

"Would it be okay with you if we made our own 'Progress over Perfection' reminder cards?" asked Indira sheepishly.

"I'd love to see that," replied Will.

After the solemn lesson on progress over perfection, the group found themselves joking and laughing again. The group finished a fabulous dinner and agreed that it had been one of the most profitable and eye-opening days they had ever spent. They thanked Will and his team, agreeing that they would stay in touch and meet again in five more years to share their progress and learning.

Chapter 5

The 10-Year Reunion

There was a noticeable buzz of conversation and laughter in the room as the doctors entered the conference room. Mal and Angie joined the group, followed by Will, who now walked with a cane and a small limp that was the result of a slight stroke he suffered last year.

The four doctors had become even better friends than they were in medical school, and they shared a certain feeling of closeness that comes from being vulnerable about the successes and challenges they had faced over the years. The synergy of the group working with Will and his team had become a force multiplier in helping them achieve their goals.

After everyone exchanged pleasantries and caught up on their lives and families, they settled into their chairs.

Will began, "Welcome, everyone! It's wonderful to see each of you today with a little more gray hair and wisdom showing. You can clearly see all my gray hair, at least what's left of it. Mal and I have enjoyed working with you over the past 10 years as each of you has charted your own path to financial independence. I am especially impressed with the amount of financial intelligence, maturity, and wisdom each of you has achieved, and am excited to have each of you share the progress and insights you've gained in your journey. Elijah, as in the past, would you like to go first?"

"Absolutely!" replied Elijah.

Each of the doctors opened the notebooks in front of them to the tab containing Elijah's results.

Elijah began, "Here is a chart showing my Investible Net Worth today and amount of retirement income I could take out at a rate of 4% if I retired now."

Elijah's Progress

Elijah's Investible Net Worth After 10 Years	
Tax-Free Retirement Accounts	$168,310
Tax-Deferred Retirement Accounts	$813,497
Taxable Investment Accounts	$543,559
Total Investments	$1,525,365
Less Deferred Income Taxes at 37%	($323,039)
Net Investible Net Worth	**$1,202,326**

Elijah explained, "At this juncture, if I continue to stay on track with my retirement investments, I should be able to retire comfortably at the age of 65."

"Good," said Serena. "I know Matt has done a good job of managing our investments." The other two doctors nodded in agreement.

Will added, "I know Matt has been working with each of you over the past 10 years. Having a good financial advisor on your team has been very beneficial for each of you, helping you avoid risky ventures and the next 'shiny object' that is always tempting to put money into."

"Serena, would you please share your progress with the group?" asked Will.

"Certainly!" replied Serena, "if you turn to my tab in your notebook, you'll find my Investible Net Worth."

Serena's Progress

Serena's Investible Net Worth After 10 Years	
Tax-Free Retirement Accounts	$869,600
Tax-Deferred Retirement Accounts	$701,290
Taxable Investment Accounts	$535,985
Total Investments	$2,106,875
Less Deferred Income Taxes at 37%	($281,216)
Net Investible Net Worth	**$1,825,660**

"If I retired today, I estimate that I would have $65,554 in after-tax annual retirement income based on the Rule of 4%. But by the age of 60, I should have accumulated enough to retire and replace my current after-tax income."

Comparing Elijah's and Serena's Investible Net Worth After 10 Years	
Serena	$1,825,660
Elijah	$1,202,326
Difference in dollars	$623,333
Difference in percentage	152%

Comparing Elijah's and Serena's After-Tax Retirement Income Using the 4% Rule at Year 10	
Serena	$65,554
Elijah	$39,579
Difference in dollars	$25,975
Difference in percentage	152%

"It's amazing how much more you can save if you are able to be an independent contractor and take advantage of all of the tax breaks available to business owners!" added Elijah.

"It's so true," replied Benjamin. "If it hadn't been for the tax planning Will and Mal provided over the years, I would not be anywhere near where I am today."

"Well then," Will said, "Don't keep us waiting any longer. Please tell us about your journey to financial independence over the past 10 years."

Benjamin replied with a sheepish smile, "Okay. Please turn in your notebook to my tab. Here are my current numbers."

Benjamin's Progress

Benjamin's Investible Net Worth After 10 Years	
Tax-Free Retirement Accounts	$869,600
Tax-Deferred Retirement Accounts	$701,290
Taxable Investment Accounts	$1,948,041
Business Interest	$310,011
Total Investments	$3,828,941
Less Deferred Income Taxes at 37%	($281,216)
Net Investible Net Worth	**$3,547,726**

Benjamin explained, "As a result of opening my second clinic last year and selling a 49% interest in my associate in the first clinic, my clinics are worth over $300,000, and I have saved and invested the net profits from the clinics."

Serena commented, "Bravo, Benjamin! You have done an incredible job of building your clinics over the past 10 years. It's shocking to see how much more net worth you have as a business owner than just an independent contractor working for someone else. Compared to my results, your net worth is almost twice mine, and your retirement income is four times what mine is!"

Comparing Serena's and Benjamin's Investible Net Worth After 10 Years	
Benjamin	$3,547,726
Serena	$1,825,660
Difference in dollars	$1,722,066
Difference in percentage	194%

Comparing Serena's and Benjamin's After-Tax Retirement Income Using the 4% Rule at Year 10	
Benjamin	$263,081
Serena	$65,554
Difference in dollars	$197,527
Difference in percentage	401%

What Accounts for Benjamin's Success Compared to Serena?

"I understand why your net worth is more than mine, but what accounts for why your retirement income is so much higher than mine at this point?" asked Serena.

Benjamin replied, "One of the biggest differences is probably because I sold a 49% interest in each of my clinics to my associate who worked in the practice. My associates were able to free me up from working in each of the clinics, and I was able to continue to receive 51% of the net profits from the clinic as somewhat passive income and roll over the savings into future clinics. The effect has a compounding effect over time, which I have started to realize over the past several years."

"At this point," Benjamin continued, "I've reached my goal of replacing my working income with passive income, but I am having so much fun I am not ready to retire. There is a lot more I would like to do! I'm only 45 years old and am not ready to retire from the practice of medicine. But at least now I can practice how I would like to practice without the stress and burnout."

Serena replied, "I am envious of your success but so happy for you!

You followed your goal of owning your own business and put in the time to learn how to be successful. You deserve your success and I hope you continue to pursue your dreams!"

Turning to Indira, Will said, "I think all of us are very excited to hear about your progress since we last met."

Elijah exclaimed, "Yes, we are!"

Indira, as she had done at the last meeting, humbly responded, "Thank you. I am so grateful to be here today with you, my dearest friends, who have been willing to share your insights and knowledge. I am very thankful for the wisdom I have received from my parents, who have been my role models since I was a child, to my sister, Mal, who has kept me on track with my goals, and my trusted advisors, Will and Matt, in helping me on my journey of financial intelligence and independence. Without all of you, I wouldn't be here today and made the progress I've made over the past 10 years. If you turn to my tab in the notebook, you'll see my numbers."

Indira's Progress

Indira's Investible Net Worth After 10 Years	
Tax-Free Retirement Accounts	$869,600
Tax-Deferred Retirement Accounts	$701,290
Taxable Investment Accounts	$2,249,316
Business Interest	$310,011
Real Estate Interest	$2,928,488
Total Investments	$7,058,705
Less Deferred Income Taxes at 37%	($281,216)
Net Investible Net Worth	**$6,777,489**

"Very impressive!" exclaimed Benjamin.

"You have once again won the gold medal. Your Investible Net Worth is almost twice mine, and your potential retirement income under the 4% Rule is one-third more than mine. You could have already retired if you wanted to!"

Comparing Benjamin's and Indira's Investible Net Worth After 10 Years	
Indira	$6,777,489
Benjamin	$3,547,726
Difference in dollars	$3,229,763
Difference in percentage	191%

Comparing Benjamin's and Indira's After-Tax Retirement Income Using the 4% Rule at Year 10	
Indira	$347,732
Benjamin	$263,081
Difference in dollars	$84,650
Difference in percentage	132%

"Thank you for your kind words," replied Indira. "Like you, I am having too much fun to retire. Frankly, I don't know what I would do if I retired now. Since we last met, I have been able to spend about a third of my time building my charitable foundation to provide medical assistance to refugees."

Will added, "And you have given more than $1 million in assistance to those refugees over the past five years."

Indira said quietly, "I have been so financially blessed that I wanted to share my success and make a difference. I did the same as Benjamin with my clinics in that I sold a 49% interest in each of them to my associates which freed my time up to do other things. Because my parents taught me the value of owning real estate, it has accounted for a big part of my financial success. I thought if I could build a successful business which could rent the real estate I acquired from me, that would give me the highest chance of achieving financial independence sooner."

"You certainly hit the ball out of the park!" Elijah exclaimed.

"You sure did, girl!" added Serena, "I am so happy for the success you have experienced at such a young age."

Step 8: Keep Perspective

"I think now might be a great time to have the last lesson," interjected Will. "Now that you are seeing the fruits of your labor, I want to talk about keeping your perspective."

"We've spent the last decade discussing and learning important lessons on how to make and keep wealth. Let me go back through the steps you've learned."

1. Develop a Written Plan
2. Reduce Taxes
3. Control Cash Flow
4. Seek Wise Counsel
5. Understand Risk
6. Build Tax-Efficient Wealth
7. Focus on Progress, Not Perfection
8. Keep Perspective

He congratulated the participants on their success in learning and applying the lessons. He also commended them for their hard work and discipline in sticking with their plans.

"It certainly wasn't easy!" Serena exclaimed as the others nodded in unison. "It was so easy to lose focus and go back to my old habits," she said.

Benjamin added, "If it hadn't been for you keeping us on track, I can't imagine how stressed I would be still working hard with not much to show for it!"

Will was happy with their feedback. "Thanks for sharing," he said. "Your experience is very common."

"However, without the last lesson, your financial intelligence and maturity will not be complete," he said.

"What I would now like to teach you is the importance of keeping the right perspective when it comes to wealth."

He started with the story of King Solomon in the Bible.

"He is considered one of the wealthiest men to have ever lived. By some estimates, he may have been worth as much as 2 trillion dollars," Will said.

"Solomon is also considered by many to be the wisest man who ever lived. He was sought out by people and rulers all over the world for his wisdom and understanding."

"Fortunately for us, King Solomon was also a prolific writer, sharing his great wisdom with all who read it. Some of you have already heard me quote from Ecclesiastes in your lessons."

He said Solomon was in a position to teach others how to have the right perspective when it came to wealth, and whether money would bring happiness.

> *He who loves money shall never have enough. The foolishness of thinking that wealth brings happiness! The more you have, the more you spend, right up to the limits of your income.* (Ecclesiastes 5:10-11, TLB)

Will told the group it was important not to be in love with creating wealth because it could result in several kinds of negative outcomes.

"Keep in mind that having wealth is not good or bad – it is morally neutral. Having the wrong perspective on money can result in pride, arrogance, stress, and greed, any one of which can destroy one's happiness and has the potential to ruin marriages and families," he said.

"The proper attitude with having wealth is one in which you remain humble and grateful, accepting that you have a responsibility to be a good steward of what you have accumulated."

He said one of the best tests of having the right perspective on money is the measure of how one gives generously to others.

"I love to tell the story of a wealthy businessman, Alfred Nobel," he said. "Randy Alcorn, in his book *The Treasure Principle*, describes an event that impacted Alfred's life":

> *Alfred Nobel dropped the newspaper and put his head in his hands. It was 1888. Nobel was a Swedish chemist who made his fortune inventing and producing dynamite. His brother Ludvig had died in France.*
>
> *But now Alfred's grief was compounded by dismay. He'd just read an obituary in a French newspaper – not*

his brother's obituary, but his! An editor had confused the brothers. The headline read, 'The Merchant of Death Is Dead.' Alfred Nobel's obituary described a man who had gotten rich by helping people kill one another.

Shaken by this appraisal of his life, Nobel resolved to use his wealth to change his legacy. When he died eight years later, he left more than $9 million to fund awards for people whose work benefited humanity. The awards became known as the Nobel Prizes.

Alfred had an opportunity to view the assessment of his life and had a chance to change it. Have you assessed what your life is invested in something of lasting value?

Will continued, "In the book, Randy tells another story that was part of a movie you may have seen, *Schindler's List*. Oskar Schindler – who bought the lives of many Jews from the Nazis – looks at his car and his gold pin and regrets that he didn't give more of his money and possessions to save more lives."

He said Schindler had used his opportunity far better than most. But in the end, he longed for a chance to go back and make better choices.

"Those are very inspiring stories," Indira exclaimed, "and I want to make sure that my life is worth something and that my legacy will be about who I helped during my lifetime here on earth, not only as a physician but as a humanitarian."

The others agreed.

"I believe that none of us have a second chance to live life over," Will answered. "We have only one opportunity – our lifetime on earth – to use our time, treasure, and talent to make a difference. I submit that one of the most effective antidotes for the potential disease of loving money is being a generous giver."

He wrapped up the meeting with personalized instructions to each of the doctors about their next 90 days and their financial independence journey in full.

The group agreed that they would stay in touch and meet again in person in several years to share their experiences and progress.

They expressed sincere appreciation and thankfulness to Will and his team for the lessons they had learned and how helpful they've been to them.

As the meeting came to an end, the four friends reflected on how radically different their personal and professional lives might have looked had they not had the good fortune of connecting with Will and his team at Provident CPAs.

Each was thankful and optimistic about the future.

Chapter 6

Epilogue

In case you are curious about how each of the friends progressed after 20 years (when each of them reached the age of 55) of beginning their journey to financial independence, here is a summary of each journey.

Elijah's Progress

Elijah's Investible Net Worth After 20 Years	
Tax-Free Retirement Accounts	$398,976
Tax-Deferred Retirement Accounts	$1,928,382
Taxable Investment Accounts	$1,288,498
Total Investments	$3,615,856
Less Deferred Income Taxes at 37%	($802,738)
Net Investible Net Worth	**$2,813,119**
After-Tax Retirement Income Using the 4% Rule	**$99,222**

Based on Matt's and Will's projections, Elijah was on track to have just in excess of $5 million in after-tax Investible Net Worth when he reaches the age of 65, which would provide him with an after-tax retirement income using the 4% Rule starting at approximately $200,000 per year.

Serena's Progress

Serena's Investible Net Worth After 20 Years	
Tax-Free Retirement Accounts	$2,061,374
Tax-Deferred Retirement Accounts	$1,662,398
Taxable Investment Accounts	$1,270,545
Total Investments	$4,994,317
Less Deferred Income Taxes at 37%	($703,080)
Net Investible Net Worth	**$4,291,237**
After-Tax Retirement Income Using the 4% Rule	**$159,899**

Serena was well on her way to retiring by the age of 60, at which time her estimated Investible Net Worth is almost $6 million, which would provide her with an after-tax retirement income of approximately $220,000 per year using the 4% Rule, which is just over her current after-tax income.

Benjamin's Progress

Benjamin's Investible Net Worth After 20 Years	
Tax-Free Retirement Accounts	$2,061,374
Tax-Deferred Retirement Accounts	$1,662,398
Taxable Investment Accounts	$6,932,235
Business Interest	$2,637,815
Total Investments	$13,293,823
Less Deferred Income Taxes at 37%	($703,080)
Net Investible Net Worth	**$12,590,742**
After-Tax Retirement Income Using the 4% Rule	**$965,492**

As mentioned in the last chapter, Benjamin had accumulated enough Investible Assets and Income to retire 10 years ago. However, he continued to grow his business by investing in an additional clinic every five years and selling 49% of each clinic to his associates.

Benjamin continued his study of business and finance. He started investing as an angel investor in start-up and growth business opportunities. Matt and Will projected that his Investible Net Worth would continue to grow to $19 million, which would generate an after-tax retirement income of $1.4 million by the age of 60. However, according to Benjamin, he would still not want to fully retire but rather continue investing and mentoring young entrepreneurial doctors on how to create wealth so that they could achieve financial independence and escape the bureaucratic healthcare industry. Benjamin enjoyed spending most of the year on his favorite beach in Puerto Rico where he moved as a resident last year to enjoy living almost completely tax-free.

Indira's Progress

Indira's Investible Net Worth After 20 Years	
Tax-Free Retirement Accounts	$2,061,374
Tax-Deferred Retirement Accounts	$1,662,398
Taxable Investment Accounts	$10,278,454
Business Interest	$2,637,815
Real Estate Interest	$9,806,858
Total Investments	$26,446,900
Less Deferred Income Taxes at 37%	($703,080)
Net Investible Net Worth	**$25,743,819**
After-Tax Retirement Income Using the 4% Rule	**$1,552,267**

Last, but certainly not least, is the story of Indira. She had achieved more financial success than she ever thought possible. Chatura is fully retired, and Indira spends most of her time working with other healthcare professionals providing medical care for refugees, and the remainder of her time managing her real estate and business investments. At her current pace, she is projected to accumulate over $41 million in Investible Net Worth and after-tax retirement income applying the 4% Rule of approximately $2.5 million annually, about 40% of which she contributes to her foundation.

Chapter 7
Getting Started

If you have made it this far, you may be wondering to yourself: Can I achieve financial independence like the doctors in this book? The answer is an unequivocal "Yes!" But it depends on how soon you get started, and whether you have the willingness to work hard and learn the principles and lessons described in the previous chapters.

At Provident CPAs, we work with hundreds of entrepreneurial doctors to help them acquire financial intelligence so that they can achieve financial independence as soon as possible. We have developed a unique model described as The Strategic Wealth System™ that focuses on three goals:

- Minimizing income taxes to the lowest amount legally possible.
- Getting control of personal and business finances.
- Optimizing tax-free and tax-efficient retirement income.

It starts with a Strategic Blueprint that is an assessment of your current situation, goals, and challenges. It also provides a personal roadmap of tax, financial, and retirement strategies. The cost is $1,250 (subject to change), but it contains a 5 times guarantee – if we cannot save you five (5) times the cost of the Strategic Blueprint in tax savings, we will refund the cost of the blueprint. You can obtain your Strategic Blueprint by logging and completing the Strategic Blueprint Starter Kit at www.therichestdoctor.com/blueprint.

You can also check out our website at www.therichestdoctor.com to subscribe to our newsletter and read our blog.

We look forward to working with you and wishing you the best of success in reaching financial independence!

CPSIA information can be obtained
at www.ICGtesting.com
Printed in the USA
BVHW041047160422
634391BV00008B/27/J